WAITING FOR CHRIST

*Meditations for Advent
and Christmas*

WAITING FOR CHRIST

*Meditations for Advent
and Christmas*

Blessed John Henry Newman

*Edited by
Christopher O. Blum*

Augustine Institute
Greenwood Village, CO

Augustine Institute
6160 S. Syracuse Way
Greenwood Village, CO 80111
Tel: (866) 767-3155
www.augustineinstitute.org

Cover design by Lisa Marie Patterson

ISBN 978-1-7325247-4-3
Library of Congress Control Number 2018954534

Printed in the United States

CONTENTS

Introduction

"A man of discernment if thou find, wait on him at daybreak, and wear out his door-step with thy frequent visiting." This sage advice, from Ronald Knox's translation of Sirach 6:36, captures the purpose of this book, which is to give its readers the chance to start each day of Advent in the company of a man of great discernment, so that Christmas will "find us more and more like him, who at this time became a little child for our sake, more simple-minded, more humble, more holy, more affectionate, more resigned, more happy, more full of God."[1]

The most celebrated of modern converts, John Henry Newman (1801–1890) was for many years a clergyman in the Church of England before being received into the Catholic Church in 1845. During his Anglican years, he won accolades for his preaching, which was as inspiring and challenging as it was captivating. Chesterton once credited Newman's style with "a magic that is like a sort of musical accompaniment," and he was afterwards lauded as "one of the greatest masters of quietly exquisite prose that the world has ever seen."[2] As to his sermons' quality as reflections on the Gospel, Richard Church, onetime Dean of St. Paul's, penned their finest praise: "They made men think of the things which the preacher spoke of, and not of the sermon or the preacher."[3] Newman's preaching realized St. Augustine's prescription that eloquence ought to be wisdom's unobtrusive companion, so that in hearing the good preacher,

---

[1] John Henry Newman, "The Mystery of Godliness," 103.
[2] G. K. Chesterton, "The Style of Newman," *The Speaker* (1904), 130–31; George Saintsbury, *A History of English Prose Rhythm* (London: Macmillan, 1922), 388.
[3] R. W. Church, *The Oxford Movement: Twelve Years, 1833–1845*, ed. G. Best (Chicago: University of Chicago Press, 1970), 92–3.

"you could almost imagine wisdom stepping out from her own house, that is from the breast of the wise man, followed by eloquence as her inseparable, even if uninvited, lady in waiting."[4]

To take the modern scalpel of the word processor to sermons of this "much-loved father of souls" may be thought an unforgiveable act of trespass.[5] It may perhaps be observed, however, that it is better for Newman to be read in part than not at all, and better that he should be appreciated by the current generation than set aside as antiquated or too difficult to be read with pleasure. My aim in presenting selections from his sermons has been to offer their essential teaching— entirely in Newman's own words—in a length and form that will make them attractive as spiritual reading. The changes I have made have chiefly consisted in selecting portions of the sermons, removing paragraphs that contained illustrations or applications ancillary to Newman's main point, bringing his text into conformity with American conventions of spelling, and changing most of his quotations of Sacred Scripture from the King James or Douay-Rheims Bibles to the Revised Standard Version, Second Catholic Edition. In addition, I have taken liberties with his punctuation, often preferring the period to the semicolon, and have on a few occasions changed a word of his to one that I thought would be more easily understood. Most of the sermons were chosen from the eight-volume Longmans' edition of his *Parochial and Plain Sermons;* some have come from other collections, such as his *Sermons on Subjects of the Day, Discourses to Mixed Congregations,* and *Sermons Preached on Various Occasions.* It is hoped that the reader of this little book will desire to read the original sermons in their entirety,

---

[4] St. Augustine, *Teaching Christianity*, trans. Edmund Hill, O.P. (Hyde Park, New York: New City Press, 1996), 206.
[5] Benedict XVI, Homily at the Mass with the Beatification of John Henry Cardinal Newman (September 19, 2010).

and will find in Blessed Cardinal Newman a worthy friend and guide for life's journey back to our Father in Heaven.

Christopher O. Blum
Augustine Institute
Greenwood Village, Colorado
Solemnity of the Assumption of the Blessed Virgin Mary, 2018

November 30

St. Andrew

The World's Benefactors

St. Andrew, who was already one of St. John's disciples, was attending on his master with another, when, as it happened, Jesus passed by. The Baptist, who had from the first declared his own subordinate place in the dispensation which was then opening, took this occasion of pointing out to his two disciples him in whom it centered. He said, "Behold the Lamb of God" (Jn 1:29). On hearing this, the two disciples immediately left John and followed Christ. He turned round and asked them "What do you seek?" (Jn 1:38). They expressed their desire to be allowed to wait upon his teaching, and he suffered them to accompany him home and to pass that day with him. What he said to them is not told us, but St. Andrew received such confirmation of the truth of the Baptist's words that in consequence he went after his own brother to tell him what he had found.

St. John the Evangelist, who has been guided to preserve various notices concerning the separate apostles which are not contained in the first three Gospels, speaks of Andrew in two other places and introduces him under circumstances which show that, little as is known of this apostle now, he was, in fact, very high in the favor and confidence of his Lord. In his twelfth chapter, he describes Andrew as bringing to Christ certain Greeks who came up to Jerusalem to worship and who were desirous of seeing him. And, what is remarkable, these strangers had first applied to St. Philip, who, though an apostle himself, instead of taking upon him to introduce them, had recourse

11

to his fellow-townsman, St. Andrew, as if, whether from age or intimacy with Christ, he was a more suitable channel for furthering their petition.

These two apostles are also mentioned together at the consultation which preceded the miracle of the loaves and fishes, and there again Andrew is engaged, as before, in the office of introducing strangers to Christ. "There is a lad here," he says to his Lord, a lad who, perhaps, had not courage to come forward of himself, "who has five barley loaves and two fish" (Jn 6:9).

The information afforded by these passages of St. Andrew's special acceptableness to Christ among the apostles is confirmed by the only place in the other Gospels, besides the catalogues, in which his name occurs. After our Lord had predicted the ruin of the Temple, "Peter and James and John and Andrew asked him privately, 'Tell us, when will this be?'" (Mk 13:3), and it was to these four that our Savior revealed the signs of his coming, and of the end of the world. Here St. Andrew is represented as in the special confidence of Christ, and associated too with those apostles whom he is known to have selected from the twelve, on various occasions, by tokens of his peculiar favor.

Little is known of St. Andrew in addition to these inspired notices of him. He is said to have preached the Gospel in Scythia, and he was at length martyred in Achaea. His death was by crucifixion, that kind of cross being used, according to the tradition, which still goes by his name.

Yet, little as Scripture tells us concerning him, it affords us enough for a lesson, and that an important one. These are the facts before us. St. Andrew was the first convert among the apostles; he was especially in our Lord's confidence; thrice is he described as introducing others to him; lastly, he is little known in history, while the place of dignity and the name of highest renown have been allotted to his brother Simon, whom he was the means of bringing to the knowledge of his Savior.

Our lesson, then, is this: that they are not necessarily the most useful in their generation, nor the most favored by God, who make the most noise in the world, and who seem to be principals in the great changes and events recorded in history. On the contrary, that even when we are able to point to a certain number of men as the real instruments of any great blessings given to mankind, our relative estimate of them, one with another, is often very erroneous. So, on the whole, if we would trace truly the hand of God in human affairs, and pursue his bounty as displayed in the world to its original sources, we must unlearn our admiration of the powerful and distinguished, our reliance on the opinion of society, our respect for the decisions of the learned or the multitude, and turn our eyes to private life, watching in all we read or witness for the true signs of God's presence, the graces of personal holiness manifested in his elect, which, weak as they may seem to mankind, are mighty through God, and have an influence upon the course of his providence, and bring about great events in the world at large, when the wisdom and strength of the natural man are of no avail.

Why indeed should we shrink from this gracious law of God's present providence in our own case, or in the case of those we love, when our subjection to it does but associate us with the best and noblest of our race, and with beings of nature and condition superior to our own? Andrew is scarcely known except by name, while Peter has ever held the place of honor all over the Church; yet Andrew brought Peter to Christ. And are not the blessed angels unknown to the world? And is not God himself, the author of all good, hid from mankind at large, partially manifested and poorly glorified in a few scattered servants here and there? And his Spirit, do we know whence it comes and whither it goes? And though he has taught me whatever there has been of wisdom among them from the beginning, yet when he came on earth in visible form, even then it was said of him "the world knew him not" (Jn 1:10). His marvelous providence works beneath a veil, which speaks but an untrue language; and to see him who is the truth and the life, we must stoop underneath it, and so in our turn hide ourselves from the world. They who present themselves at kings' courts pass on to the inner chambers, where the gaze of the rude multitude cannot pierce. And we, if we would see the King of kings in his glory, must be content to disappear from the things that are seen. Hid are the saints of God. If they are known to man, it is accidentally, in their temporal offices, as holding some high earthly station, or effecting some mere civil work, not as saints. St. Peter has a place in history, far more as a chief instrument of a strange revolution in human affairs than in his true character as a self-denying follower of his Lord, to whom truths were revealed which flesh and blood could not discern.

December 1

Worship, a Preparation for Christ's Coming

Each new year, as it passes, brings us the same warnings again and again, and none perhaps more impressive than those with which it comes to us at this season. The very frost and cold, rain and gloom, which now befall us, forebode the last dreary days of the world, and in religious hearts raise the thought of them. The year is worn out. Spring, summer, autumn, each in turn, have brought their gifts and done their utmost, but they are over, and the end is come. All is past and gone; all has failed. We are tired of the past; we would not have the seasons longer; and the austere weather which succeeds, though ungrateful to the body, is in tune with our feelings, and acceptable. Such is the frame of mind which befits the end of the year, and such the frame of mind which comes alike on good and bad at the end of life. The days have come in which they have no pleasure; yet they would hardly be young again, could they be so by wishing it. Life is well enough in its way, but it does not satisfy. Thus the soul is cast forward upon the future, and in proportion as its conscience is clear and its perception keen and true does it rejoice solemnly that "the night is far gone, the day is at hand" (Rom 13:12), that there are "a new heaven and a new earth" (Rev 21:1) to come, though the former are failing. Nay, rather that, because they are failing, it will soon "see the King in his beauty" and "behold a land that stretches afar" (Is 33:17). These are feelings for holy men in winter and in age, waiting, in some dejection perhaps, but with comfort on the whole, and calmly though earnestly, for the advent of Christ.

And such, too, are the feelings with which we now come before him in prayer day by day. The season is chill and dark, and the breath of the morning is damp, and worshippers are few, but all this befits those who are by profession penitents and mourners, watchers and pilgrims. More dear to them that loneliness, more cheerful that severity, and more bright that gloom, than all those aids and appliances of luxury by which men nowadays attempt to make prayer less disagreeable to them. True faith does not covet comforts. It only complains when it is forbidden to kneel, when it reclines upon cushions, is protected by curtains, and encompassed by warmth. Its only hardship is to be hindered, or to be ridiculed, when it would place itself as a sinner before its judge. They who realize that awful day when they shall see him face to face, whose eyes are as a flame of fire, will as little bargain to pray pleasantly now as they will think of doing so then.

One year goes and then another, but the same warnings recur. The frost or rain comes again; the earth is stripped of its brightness; there is nothing to rejoice in. And then, amid this unprofitableness of earth and sky, the well-known words return: the prophet Isaiah is read, the same epistle and Gospel bidding us "to wake from sleep" (Rom 13:11) and welcome him "who comes in the name of the Lord" (Mt 21:9), the same prayers, beseeching him to prepare us for judgment. O blessed they who obey these warning voices, and look out for him whom they have not seen, because they "have loved his appearing" (2 Tim 4:8).

We cannot have fitter reflections at this season than these. What may be the destiny of other orders of beings we know not, but this we know to be our own fearful lot, that before us lies a time when we must have the sight of our Maker and Lord face to face. We know not what is reserved for other beings; there may be some, which, knowing nothing of their Maker, are never to be brought before him. For what we can tell, this may be the case with the brute creation. It may be the law of their nature that they should live and die, or live on an indefinite period, upon the very outskirts of his government, sustained by him, but never permitted to know or approach him. But this is not our case. We are destined to come before him, nay, and to come before him in judgment, and that on our first meeting, and that suddenly. We are not merely to be rewarded or punished; we are to be judged. Recompense is to come upon our actions, not by a mere general provision or course of nature, as it does at present, but from the lawgiver himself in person. We have to stand before his righteous presence, and that one by one. One by one we shall have to endure his holy and searching eye. At present, we are in a world of shadows. What we see is not substantial. Suddenly it will be rent in twain and vanish away, and our Maker will appear. He will look on us, while we look on him.

December 2

Waiting for Christ

The substance of religion consists in faith, hope, and charity, and the qualification for eternal life is to be in a state of grace and free from mortal sin. Yet, when we come to the question, how we are to preserve ourselves in a state of grace and gain the gift of perseverance in it, then a number of observances have claims upon us, over and above those duties in which the substance of religion lies, as being its safeguard and protection. And these same observances, as being of a nature to catch the eye of the world, become the badges of the Christian, as contrasted with other men, whereas faith, hope, and charity are lodged deep in the breast, and are not seen. Now, one of these characteristics of a Christian spirit, springing from the three theological virtues, and then in turn defending and strengthening them, is that habit of waiting and watching, to which this season of the year especially invites us; and the same habit is also a mark of the children of the Church, and a note of her divine origin.

We read in the Gospel that our Lord on one occasion "entered a village" and was received and entertained by "a woman named Martha." There were two sisters, Martha and Mary. "Martha was distracted with much serving;" but Mary sat at our Lord's feet, and heard his words. You recollect his comparison of these two holy sisters, one with another. "Martha, Martha," he said, "you are anxious and troubled about many things; one thing is needful. Mary has chosen the good portion." Now Martha loved him, and Mary loved him; but Mary waited on him too, and therefore had the promise of perseverance held up to her: "Mary has chosen the good portion, which shall not be taken away from her" (Lk 10:38-42).

They, then, watch and wait for their Lord, who are tender and sensitive in their devotion towards him, who feed on the thought of him, hang on his words, live in his smile, and thrive and grow under his hand. They are eager for his approval, quick in catching his meaning, jealous of his honor. They see him in all things, expect him in all events, and amid all the cares, the interests, and the pursuits of this life, still would feel an awful joy, not a disappointment, did they hear that he was on the point of coming. "By night I sought him whom my soul loves," says the inspired canticle; "I sought him but found him not.... I will rise now, and go about the city, in the streets and in the squares; I will seek him" (Sg 3:1-2).

Must I be more definite in my description of this affectionate temper? I ask, then, do you know the feeling of expecting a friend, expecting him to come, and he delays? Do you know what it is to be in the company of those with whom you are not at your ease, and to wish the time to pass away, and the hour to strike when you are to be released from them? Do you know what it is to be in anxiety lest something should happen, which may happen, or may not; or to be in suspense about some important event, which makes your heart beat when anything reminds you of it, and of which you think the first thing in the morning? Do you know what it is to have friends in a distant country, to expect news from them, and to wonder from day to day what they are doing, and whether they are well? Do you know what it is so to love and live upon a person who is present with you, that your eyes follow his, that you read his soul, that you see its changes in his countenance, that you anticipate his wants, that you are sad in his sadness, troubled when he is vexed, restless when you cannot understand him, relieved, comforted, when you have cleared up the mystery?

This intimate, immediate dependence on Emmanuel, God with us, has been in all ages the characteristic, almost the definition, of a Christian. It is the ordinary feeling of Catholic populations; it is the elementary feeling of everyone who has but a common hope of heaven. I recollect years ago, hearing an acquaintance, not a Catholic, speak of a work of devotion, written as Catholics usually write, with wonder and perplexity, because, he said, the author wrote as if he had a sort of personal attachment to our Lord; it was as if he had seen him, known him, lived with him, instead of merely professing and believing the great doctrine of the Atonement. It is this same phenomenon which strikes those who are not Catholics when they enter our churches. They themselves are accustomed to do religious acts simply as a duty; they are serious at prayer time, and behave with decency, because it is a duty. But you know, mere duty, a sense of propriety, and good behavior, these are not the ruling principles present in the minds of worshippers. Wherefore, on the contrary, those spontaneous postures of devotion? Why those unstudied gestures? Why those abstracted countenances? Why that heedlessness of the presence of others? The spectator sees the effect; he cannot understand the cause of it. Why is this simple earnestness of worship? We have no difficulty in answering. It is because the Incarnate Savior is present in the tabernacle. And then, when suddenly the hitherto silent church is, as it were, illuminated with the full piercing burst of voices from the whole congregation, it is because he now has gone up upon his throne over the altar, there to be adored.

December 3

St. Francis Xavier

The Ventures of Faith

"They said to him, 'We are able'" (Mt 20:22). These words of
the holy apostles James and John were in reply to a very solemn
question addressed to them by their Divine Master. They
coveted, with a noble ambition, though as yet unpracticed in
the highest wisdom, untaught in the holiest truth, they coveted
to sit beside him on his throne of glory. They would be content
with nothing short of that special gift which he had come to
grant to his elect, which he shortly after died to purchase for
them, and which he offers to us. They ask the gift of eternal
life, and he in answer told them, not that they should have
it (though for them it was really reserved), but he reminded
them what they must venture for it: "'Are you able to drink the
chalice that I am to drink?' They said to him, 'We are able.'"
Here then a great lesson is impressed upon us, that our duty
as Christians lies in this, in making ventures for eternal life
without the absolute certainty of success.

Success and reward everlasting they will have, who persevere
unto the end. Doubt we cannot, that the ventures of all Christ's
servants must be returned to them at the Last Day with abundant
increase. This is a true saying: he returns far more than we lend
to him, and without fail. But I am speaking of individuals, of
ourselves one by one. No one among us knows for certain that
he himself will persevere; yet everyone among us, to give himself
even a chance of success at all, must make a venture. As regards
individuals, then, it is quite true, that all of us must for certain
make ventures for heaven, yet without the certainty of success

through them. This, indeed, is the very meaning of the word *venture*; for that is a strange venture which has nothing in it of fear, risk, danger, anxiety, uncertainty. Yes, so it certainly is. And in this consists the excellence and nobleness of faith. This is the very reason why faith is singled out from other graces, and honored as the special means of our justification: its presence implies that we have the heart to make a venture.

If then faith be the essence of a Christian life, it follows that our duty lies in risking upon Christ's word what we have, for what we have not; and doing so in a noble, generous way, not indeed rashly or lightly, still without knowing accurately what we are doing, not knowing either what we give up, nor again what we shall gain; uncertain about our reward, uncertain about our extent of sacrifice, in all respects leaning, waiting upon him, trusting in him to fulfil his promise, trusting in him to enable us to fulfil our own vows, and so in all respects proceeding without carefulness or anxiety about the future.

For instance: St. Barnabas had a property in Cyprus; he gave it up for the poor of Christ. Here is an intelligible sacrifice. He did something he would not have done, unless the Gospel were true. It is plain, if the Gospel turned out a fable (which God forbid), but if so, he would have taken his line most unskillfully; he would be in a great mistake, and would have suffered a loss. He would be like a merchant whose vessels were wrecked, or whose correspondents had failed. Man has confidence in man, he trusts to the credit of his neighbor, but Christians do not risk largely upon their Savior's word. And this is the one thing they have to do. Christ tells us himself, "And I tell you, make friends for yourselves by means of unrighteous mammon, so that when it fails they may receive you into the eternal habitations" (Lk 16:9); that is, buy an interest in the next world with that wealth which this world uses unrighteously: feed the hungry, clothe the naked, relieve the sick, and it shall turn to "purses that do not grow old, with a treasure in the heavens that does not fail" (Lk 12:33). Thus almsdeeds, I say, are an intelligible venture and an evidence of faith.

So again the man who, when his prospects in the world are good, gives up the promise of wealth or of eminence in order to be nearer Christ, to have a place in his temple, to have more opportunity for prayer and praise, he makes a sacrifice.

Or he who, from a noble striving after perfection, puts off the desire of worldly comforts, and is, like Daniel or St. Paul, in much labor and business, yet with a solitary heart he too ventures something upon the certainty of the world to come.

Or he who, after falling into sin, repents in deed as well as in word, puts some yoke upon his shoulder, subjects himself to punishment, is severe upon his flesh, denies himself innocent pleasures, or puts himself to public shame: he too shows that his faith is the realizing of things hoped for, the warrant of things not seen.

Or again: he who only gets himself to pray against those things which the many seek after, and to embrace what the heart naturally shrinks from; he who, when God's will seems to tend towards worldly ill, while he deprecates it, yet prevails on himself to say heartily, "Thy will be done;" he, even, is not without his sacrifice. Or he who, being in prospect of wealth, honestly prays God that he may never be rich; or he who is in prospect of station, and earnestly prays that he may never have it. Or he who has friends or kindred, and acquiesces with an entire heart in their removal while it is yet doubtful, who can say, "Take them away, if it be your will, to you I give them up, to you I commit them," and is willing to be taken at his word: he too risks somewhat, and is accepted.

Alas! that we, my brethren, have not more of this high and unearthly spirit! How is it that we are so contented with things as they are, that we are so willing to be let alone, and to enjoy this life, that we make such excuses, if any one presses on us the necessity of something higher, the duty of bearing the cross, if we would earn the crown, of the Lord Jesus Christ?

I repeat it: what are our ventures and risks upon the truth of his word? For he says expressly, "Every one who has left houses or brothers or sisters or father or mother or children or lands, for my name's sake, will receive a hundredfold, and inherit eternal life" (Mt 19:29).

December 4
St. John of Damascus

Truth Hidden When Not Sought After

Nothing is more common than to think that we shall gain religious knowledge as a thing of course, without express trouble on our part. Though there is no art or business of this world which is learned without time and exertion, yet it is commonly conceived that the knowledge of God and our duty will come as if by accident or by a natural process. Men go by their feelings and likings; they take up what is popular, or what comes first to hand. They think it much if they now and then have serious thoughts, if they now and then open the Bible; and their minds recur with satisfaction to such seasons, as if they had done some very great thing, never remembering that to seek and gain religious truth is a long and systematic work. They say that religious truth is simple and easily acquired; that Scripture, being intended for all, is at once open to all; and that if it had difficulties, that very circumstance would be an objection to it.

In these and other ways do men deceive themselves into a carelessness about religious truth. And is not all this varied negligence sufficient to account for the varieties of religious opinion which we see all around us? Do not these two facts illustrate each other: the discordance of our religious opinions needing some explanation, and our actual indolence and negligence in seeking the truth accounting for it?

No one who does not seek the truth with all his heart and strength can tell what is of importance and what is not. "Seek, and you will find" (Mt 7:7); this is the Divine rule. "If you cry out for insight and raise your voice for understanding, if you seek it like silver and search for it as for hidden treasures; then you will understand the fear of the Lᴏʀᴅ and find the knowledge of God" (Prv 2:3-5).

This is a subject which cannot too strongly be insisted on. Act up to your light, though in the midst of difficulties, and you will be carried on, you do not know how far. Abraham obeyed the call and journeyed, not knowing whither he went. So we, if we follow the voice of God, shall be brought on step by step into a new world, of which before we had no idea. This is his gracious way with us: he gives, not all at once, but by measure and season, wisely. "To him who has will more be given" (Mt 13:12). But we must begin at the beginning. Each truth has its own order; we cannot join the way of life at any point of the course we please; we cannot learn advanced truths before we have learned primary ones. "Call to me," says the divine Word, "and I will answer you, and will tell you great and hidden things which you have not known" (Jer 33:3). Religious men are always learning; but when men refuse to profit by light already granted, their light is turned to darkness. Observe our Lord's conduct with the Pharisees. They asked him on what authority he acted. He gave them no direct answer, but referred them to the mission of John the Baptist: "The baptism of John., where was it from? From heaven or from men?" (Mt 21:25). They refused to say. Then he said, "Neither will I tell you by what authority I do these things" (Mt 21:27). That is, they would not profit by the knowledge they already had from St. John the Baptist, who spoke of Christ, therefore no more was given them.

All of us may learn a lesson here, for all of us are in danger of hastily finding fault with others and condemning their opinions or practices, not considering that unless we have faithfully obeyed our conscience and improved our talents, we are no fit judges of them at all. Christ and his saints are alike destitute of form or comeliness in the eyes of the world, and it is only as we labor to change our nature, through God's help, and to serve him truly, that we begin to discern the beauty of holiness.

There must be a right and a wrong, and no matter whether others agree with us or not, it is to us a solemn practical concern not to turn away our ears from the truth. Let not the diversity of opinion in the world dismay you, or deter you from seeking all your life long true wisdom. It is not a search for this day or that, but as you should ever grow in grace, so should you ever grow also in the knowledge of our Lord and Savior Jesus Christ. Care not for the perplexing question which many will put to you, "How can you be sure that you are right more than others?" Others are nothing to you, if they are not holy and devout. And we all know what is meant by being holy; we know whom we should call holy. To be holy is to be like an apostle. Seek truth in the way of obedience; try to act up to your conscience, and let your opinions be the result, not of mere chance reasoning or fancy, but of an improved heart. This way carries with it an evidence to ourselves of its being the right way, if any way be right; and that there is a right and a wrong way conscience also tells us. God surely will listen to none but those who strive to obey him.

I know we shall find it very hard to rouse ourselves, to break the force of habit, to resolve to serve God and persevere in doing so. And assuredly we must expect, even at best, and with all our efforts, perhaps backslidings, and certainly much continual imperfection all through our lives, in all we do. But this should create in us a horror of disobedience, not a despair at overcoming ourselves. We are not under the law of nature, but under grace; we are not bid do a thing above our strength, because, though our hearts are naturally weak, we are not left to ourselves. According to the command, so is the gift. God's grace is sufficient for us. Why, then, should we fear? Rather, why should we not make any sacrifice, and give up all that is naturally pleasing to us, rather than that light and truth should have come into the world, yet we not find them? Let us be willing to endure toil and trouble. And should times of comparative quiet be given to us, should for a while temptation be withdrawn, or the Spirit of comfort poured upon us, let us not inconsiderately rest in these accidental blessings. We live here to struggle and to endure. The time of eternal rest will come hereafter. "Blessed are those whose way is blameless, who walk in the law of the Lord! Blessed are those who keep his testimonies, who seek him with their whole heart" (Ps 119:1-2).

December 5

Reverence, a Belief in God's Presence

Who is there to deny that if we saw God, we should fear? Take the most cold and secular of all those who explain away the Gospel, or take the most heated and fanatic of those who consider it peculiarly their own: would either party keep from fearing greatly if they saw God? Surely it is quite a truism to say that any creature would fear. But why would he fear? Would it be merely because he saw God, or because he knew that God was present? If he shut his eyes, he would still fear, for his eyes had conveyed to him this solemn truth: to have seen would be enough. But if so, does it not follow at once, that, if men do not fear, it is because they do not act as they would act if they saw him, that is, they do not feel that he is present? Is it not quite certain that men would not use Almighty God's name so freely, if they thought he was really in hearing, nay, close beside them when they spoke?

And so of those other instances of want of godly fear, they come from deadness to the presence of God. If a man believes him present, he will shrink from addressing him familiarly, or using before him unreal words, or peremptorily and on his own judgment deciding what God's will is, or claiming his confidence, or addressing him in a familiar posture of body. Take the man who is most confident that he has nothing to fear from the presence of God, and that Almighty God is at peace with him, and place him actually before the throne of God: would he have no misgivings? And will he dare to say that those misgivings are a weakness, a mere irrational perturbation, which he ought not to feel?

This will be seen more clearly, by considering how differently we feel towards and speak of our friends as present or absent. Their presence is a check upon us. It acts as an external law, compelling us to do or not do what we should not do or do otherwise, or should do but for it. This is just what most men lack in their religion at present: such an external restraint arising from the consciousness of God's presence. Consider how differently we speak of a friend, however intimate, when present or absent; consider how we feel, should it so happen that we have begun to speak of him as if he were not present, on finding suddenly that he is. There is a tone of voice and a manner of speaking about persons absent, which we should consider disrespectful, or at least inconsiderate, if they were present. When that is the case, we are ever thinking, even if unconsciously to ourselves, how they will take what we say, how it will affect them, what they will say to us or think of us in turn. When a person is absent, we are tempted perhaps confidently to say what his opinion is on certain points; but should he be present, we qualify our words. We hardly like to speak at all, from the vivid consciousness that we may be wrong, and that he is present to tell us so. We are very cautious of pronouncing what his feelings are on the matter in hand, or how he is disposed towards ourselves, and in all things we observe a deference and delicacy in our conduct towards him.

Now, if we feel this towards our fellows, what shall we feel in the presence of an angel? And if so, what in the presence of the all-knowing, all-searching judge of men? What is respect and consideration in the case of our fellows, becomes godly fear as regards Almighty God. And they who do not fear him, in one word, do not believe that he sees and hears them. If they did, they would cease to boast so confidently of his favorable thoughts of them, to foretell his dealings, to pronounce upon his revelations, to make free with his name, and to address him familiarly.

Enough has been said now to show that godly fear must be a duty, if to live in God's presence is a duty. It must be a privilege of the Gospel, if the spiritual sight of "the king in his beauty" (Is 33:17) be one of its privileges. Fear follows from faith necessarily, as would be plain, even though there were not a text in the Bible saying so. But in fact, as it is scarcely needful to say, Scripture abounds in precepts to fear God. Such as the words of the wise man: "The fear of the LORD is the beginning of knowledge" (Prv 1:7). Such as the words of St. Paul, who, in like manner, after having discoursed at length upon faith as "the assurance of things hoped for, the conviction of things not seen" (Heb 11:1), adds: "Let us offer to God acceptable worship, with reverence and awe" (Heb 12:28). Such as St. Luke's account of the Church militant on earth, that "walking in the fear of the Lord and in the comfort of the Holy Spirit, it was multiplied" (Acts 9:31). Such as St. John's account of the Church triumphant in heaven: "Who shall not fear," they say, "and glorify your name, O Lord?" (Rev 15:4). And now, if this be so, can anything be clearer than that the want of fear is nothing else but want of faith, and that in consequence we in this age are approaching in religious temper that evil day of which it is said, "When the Son of man comes, will he find faith on earth?" (Lk 18:8). Is it wonderful that we have no fear in our words and mutual intercourse, when we exercise no acts of faith?

What, you will ask, are acts of faith? Such as these: to come often to prayer is an act of faith; to kneel down instead of sitting is an act of faith; to strive to attend to your prayers is an act of faith; to behave in God's house otherwise than you would in a common room is an act of faith; to come to it on weekdays as well as Sundays is an act of faith; to come often to the most holy sacrament is an act of faith, and to be still and reverent during that sacred service is an act of faith. These are all acts of faith, because they all are acts such as we should perform, if we saw and heard him who is present, though with our bodily eyes we see and hear him not. But "blessed are those who have not seen, and yet believe" (Jn 20:29), for, be sure, if we thus act, we shall, through God's grace, be gradually imbued with the spirit of his holy fear. We shall in time, in our mode of talking and acting, in our religious services and our daily conduct, manifest, not with constraint and effort, but spontaneously and naturally, that we fear him while we love him.

December 6

St. Nicholas

The Weapons of Saints

Strength, numbers, wealth, philosophy, eloquence, craft, experience of life, knowledge of human nature: these are the means by which worldly men have ever gained the world. But in that kingdom which Christ has set up, all is contrariwise. "The weapons of our warfare are not worldly but have divine power to destroy strongholds" (2 Cor 10:4). What before was in honor, has been dishonored; what before was in dishonor, has come to honor; what before was successful, fails; what before failed, succeeds. What before was great, has become little; what before was little, has become great. Weakness has conquered strength, for the hidden strength of God "is made perfect in weakness" (2 Cor 12:9). Death has conquered life, for in that death is a more glorious resurrection. Spirit has conquered flesh, for that spirit is an inspiration from above. A new kingdom has been established, not merely different from all kingdoms before it, but contrary to them: a paradox in the eyes of man, the visible rule of the invisible Savior.

Such is the kingdom of the sons of God, and while it endures, there is ever a supernatural work going on by which all that man thinks great is overcome, and what he despises prevails.

Yes, so it is. Since Christ sent down gifts from on high, the saints are ever taking possession of the kingdom, and with the weapons of saints. The invisible powers of the heavens—truth, meekness, and righteousness—are ever coming in upon the earth, ever pouring in, gathering, thronging, warring, triumphing, under the guidance of him "who died and came to life" (Rev 2:8).

Now let us apply this great truth to ourselves, for be it ever recollected: we are the sons of God, we are the soldiers of Christ. The kingdom is within us, and among us, and around us. We are apt to speak of it as a matter of history, but really we are a part of it, or ought to be. And, as we wish to be a living portion of it, which is our only hope of salvation, we must learn what its characters are in order to imitate them. It is the characteristic of Christ's Church that the first should be last and the last first.

We have most of us by nature longings more or less, and aspirations after something greater than this world can give. Youth, especially, has a natural love for what is noble and heroic. We like to hear marvelous tales which throw us out of things as they are and introduce us to things that are not. We love to fancy ourselves involved in circumstances of danger or trial and acquitting ourselves well under them. Such is the state of young persons before the world alters them, before the world comes upon them with its withering, debasing, deadening influence, before it breathes on them and blights and parches and strips off their green foliage, and leaves them as dry and wintry trees without sap or sweetness. But before that time, they have desires after things above this world. While their hearts are thus unsettled, Christ comes to them, if they will receive him, and promises to satisfy their great need, this hunger and thirst which wearies them. He does not wait till they have learned to ridicule high feelings as mere romantic dreams. He comes to the young. He has them baptized, and then promises them, and in a higher way, those unknown blessings which they yearn after. He seems to say, in the words of the apostle, "What therefore you worship as unknown, this I proclaim to you" (Acts 17:23). You are seeking what you see not, I give it to you; you desire to be great, I will make you so. But observe how: just in the reverse way to what you expect. The way to real glory is to become unknown and despised.

He says to the aspiring: "Whoever would be great among you must be your servant, and whoever would be first among you must be your slave; even as the Son of man came not to be served but to serve" (Mt 20:26-28). Here is our rule. The way to mount up is to go down. Every step we take downward makes us higher in the kingdom of heaven. Do you desire to be great? Make yourselves little. If you minister to the humble and despised, if you feed the hungry, tend the sick, succor the distressed; if you bear with the ill-tempered, submit to insult, endure ingratitude, render good for evil, you are, as by a divine charm, getting power over the world and rising among the creatures. God has established this law. Thus he does his wonderful works. His instruments are poor and despised; the world hardly knows their names. They rise by falling. Plainly so, for no condescension can be so great as that of our Lord himself. The more they abase themselves, the more like they are to him; and the more like they are to him, the greater must be their power with him.

Let us then understand our place as the redeemed children of God. Some must be great in this world, but woe to those who make themselves great; woe to any who take one step out of their way with this object before them. Let this be the settled view of all who would promote Christ's cause upon earth: our warfare is not with carnal weapons, but with heavenly. The world does not understand what our real power is and where it lies. And until we put ourselves into its hands of our own actions, it can do nothing against us. Till we leave off patience, meekness, purity, resignation, and peace, it can do nothing against that truth which is our birthright, that cause which is ours, as it has been the cause of all saints before us.

This be our duty in the dark night, while we wait for the day, while we wait for him who is our day, while we wait for his coming, who is gone, who will return, and before whom all the tribes of the earth will mourn, but the sons of God will rejoice. "It does not yet appear what we shall be, but we know that when he appears we shall be like him, for we shall see him as he is. And everyone who thus hopes in him purifies himself as he is pure" (1 Jn 3:2-3). It is our blessedness to be made like the all-holy, all-gracious, long-suffering, and merciful God, who made and who redeemed us, in whose presence is perfect rest and perfect peace, whom the Seraphim are harmoniously praising, and the Cherubim tranquilly contemplating, and angels silently serving, and the Church thankfully worshipping. All is order, repose, love, and holiness in heaven. There is no anxiety, no ambition, no resentment, no discontent, no bitterness, no remorse, no tumult. "You keep him in perfect peace, whose mind is stayed on you, because he trusts in you. Trust in the LORD forever, for the LORD God is an everlasting rock" (Is 26:3-4).

December 7

St. Ambrose

Christian Nobleness

Religious men, knowing what great things have been done for them, cannot but grow greater in mind in consequence. We know how power and responsibility change men in matters of this world. They become more practical, more decisive. They fear to commit mistakes, yet they dare more because they have a consciousness of liberty and power and an opportunity for great successes. And thus the Christian, even in the way of nature, without speaking of the influence of heavenly grace upon him, cannot but change from the state of children to that of men, when he understands his own privileges. The more he knows and fears the gift committed to him, so much the more reverent is he towards himself, as being put in charge with it.

Consider the language in which our Lord and his apostles describe the gift: "If a man loves me," says Christ, "he will keep my word, and my Father will love him, and we will come to him and make our home with him" (Jn 14:23). Again, in St. Paul's words, "We are the temple of the living God; as God said, 'I will live in them and move among them'" (2 Cor 6:16). Again, "Do you not know that your body is a temple of the Holy Spirit within you, which you have from God? You are not your own" (1 Cor 6:19). And St. John, "Whoever confesses that Jesus is the Son of God, God abides in him, and he in God" (1 Jn 4:15). Is it not plain that such a doctrine will raise the Christian above himself, and, without impairing—nay, even while increasing his humility—will make him feel all things of earth as little, and of small interest or account, and will preserve him from the agitations of mind which they naturally occasion?

Christians are called upon to think little of the ordinary objects which men pursue: wealth, luxury, distinction, popularity, and power. It was this negligence about the world which brought upon them in primitive times the reproach of being indolent. Their heathen enemies spoke truly: indolent and indifferent they were about temporal matters. If the goods of this world came in their way, they were not bound to decline them, nor would they forbid others in the religious use of them, but they thought them vanities, the toys of children, which serious men let drop. Nay, St. Paul betrays the same feeling as regards our temporal callings and states generally. After discoursing about them, suddenly he breaks off as if impatient of the multitude of words: "I mean, brethren, the appointed time has grown very short" (1 Cor 7:29).

Hence, too, the troubles of life gradually affect the Christian less and less, as his view of his own real blessedness, under the dispensation of the Spirit, grows upon him; and even though persecuted, to take an extreme case, he knows well that, through God's inward presence, he is greater than those who for the time have power over him, as martyrs and confessors have often shown. And, in like manner, he will be calm and collected under all circumstances; he will make light of injuries, and forget them from mere contempt of them. He will be undaunted, as fearing God more than man; he will be firm in faith and consistent, as "seeing him who is invisible" (Heb 11:27).

And now, further, let it be observed that all this greatness of mind which in other religious systems degenerates into pride is in the Gospel compatible—nay, rather, intimately connected—with the deepest humility. It is true, that, so great are the Christian privileges, there is serious danger lest common men should be puffed up by them; but this will be when persons take them to themselves who have no right to them. Surely they who pride themselves on the gift have forgotten the very elements of the Gospel of Christ. They have forgotten that the gift is not only "a fragrance from life to life" but "from death to death" (2 Cor 2:16); that it is possible to "outrage the Spirit of grace" (Heb 10:29); and that "it is impossible to restore again to repentance those who have once been enlightened, who have tasted the heavenly gift, and have become partakers of the Holy Spirit" (Heb 6:4). Again, if they do anything well, "what have you that you did not receive?" (1 Cor 4:7). St. Paul shows us how we should feel about God's gifts, and how to boast without pride, when he first says, "I worked harder than any of them" and then adds "though it was not I, but the grace of God which is with me" (1 Cor 15:10).

Accordingly, the self-respect of a Christian is no personal and selfish feeling, but rather a principle of loyal devotion and reverence towards that Divine Master who condescends to visit him. He acts, not hastily, but under restraint and fearfully, as understanding that God's eye is over him, and God's hand upon him, and God's voice within him. He acts with the recollection that his omniscient guide is also his future judge, and that while he moves him, he is also noting down in his book how he answers to his godly motions. He acts with a memory laden with past infirmity and sin, and a consciousness that he has much more to mourn over and repent of, in the years gone by, than to rejoice in. It is one thing not to trust in the world; it is another thing to trust in one's self.

Let those who have had seasons of seriousness, lengthen them into a life. Let those who have hitherto lived religiously, learn devotion. Let those who have lived in good conscience, learn to live by faith. Let those who have made a good profession, aim at consistency. Let those who take pleasure in religious worship, aim at inward sanctity. Let those who have knowledge, learn to love, and let those who meditate, forget not mortification. Let not this sacred season leave us as it found us. Let it leave us, not as children, but as heirs and as citizens of the kingdom of heaven. The time may come when we shall desire to see one of the days of the Son of man, and see it not. Let us redeem the time while it is called today, "until we all attain to the unity of the faith and of the knowledge of the Son of God, to mature manhood, to the measure of the stature of the fulness of Christ" (Eph 4:13).

December 8

The Immaculate Conception

The Glories of Mary for the Sake of Her Son

When the Eternal Word decreed to come on earth, he did not work by halves, but he came to be a man like any of us, to take a human soul and body, and to make them his own. The world allows that God is man; the admission costs it little, for God is everywhere, and (as it may say) is everything; but it shrinks from confessing that God is the Son of Mary. It shrinks, for it is at once confronted with a severe fact, which violates and shatters its own unbelieving view of things. The revealed doctrine forthwith takes its true shape and receives historical reality, and the Almighty is introduced into his own world at a certain time and in a definite way. Dreams are broken and shadows depart. The Divine truth is no longer a poetical expression, or a devotional exaggeration, or a mystical economy, or a mythical representation. "Sacrifices and offerings," the shadows of the Law, "you have not desired, but a body have you prepared for me" (Heb 10:5). "That which was from the beginning, which we have heard, which we have seen with our eyes, which we have looked upon and touched with our hands" (1 Jn 1:1), such is the record of the apostle, in opposition to those who denied that "Jesus Christ has come in the flesh" (1 Jn 4:2). And the confession that Mary is the Mother of God is that safeguard wherewith we seal up and secure the doctrine of the apostle from all evasion. It declares that he is God; it implies that he is man; it suggests to us that he is God still, though he has become man, and that he is true man though he is God. By witnessing the process of the union, it secures the reality of the two subjects of the unity, the divinity and the manhood. If Mary is the Mother of God, Christ must be literally Emmanuel, God with us.

Mary is exalted for the sake of Jesus. It was fitting that she, as being a creature, though the first of creatures, should have an office of ministration. She, as others, came into the world to do a work, she had a mission to fulfill; her grace and her glory are not for her own sake, but for her Maker's; and to her is committed the custody of the Incarnation. This is her appointed office. "A Virgin shall conceive, and bear a Son, and shall call his name Emmanuel" (Is 7:14).

It would not have sufficed in order to bring out and impress on us the idea that God is man had his mother been an ordinary person. A mother without a home in the Church, without dignity, without gifts, would have been, as far as the defense of the Incarnation goes, no mother at all. She would not have remained in the memory or the imagination of men. If she is to witness and remind the world that God became man, she must be on a high and eminent station for the purpose. She must be made to fill the mind, in order to suggest the lesson. When she once attracts our attention, she begins to preach Jesus. "Why should she have such prerogatives," we ask, "unless he be God?" This is why she has other prerogatives besides, namely, the gifts of personal purity and intercessory power, distinct from her maternity. She is personally endowed that she may perform her office well. She is exalted in herself that she may minister to Christ.

Mary, then, is a specimen, and more than a specimen, in the purity of her soul and body, of what man was before his fall, and what he would have been, had he risen to his full perfection. The course of ages was to be reversed; the tradition of evil was to be broken; a gate of light was to be opened amid the darkness, for the coming of the Just; a Virgin conceived and bore him.

It was fitting, for his honor and glory, that she, who was the instrument of his bodily presence, should first be a miracle of his grace. It was fitting that she should triumph, where Eve had failed, and should bruise the serpent's head (cf. Gn 3:15) by the spotlessness of her sanctity. In some respects, indeed, the curse was not reversed. Mary came into a fallen world and resigned herself to its laws; she, as also the son she bore, was exposed to pain of soul and body, she was subjected to death. But she was not put under the power of sin. As grace was infused into Adam from the first moment of his creation, so that he never had experience of his natural poverty till sin reduced him to it, so was grace given from the first in still ampler measure to Mary, and she never incurred, in fact, Adam's deprivation. She began where others end, whether in knowledge or in love. She was from the first clothed in sanctity, destined for perseverance, luminous and glorious in God's sight, and incessantly employed in meritorious acts, which continued till her last breath. Hers was emphatically "the path of the righteous," which is "like the light of dawn, which shines brighter and brighter until full day" (Prov 4:18), and, sinlessness in thought, word, and deed, in small things as well as great, in venial matters as well as grievous, is surely but the natural and obvious sequel of such a beginning. If Adam might have kept himself from sin in his first state, much more shall we expect immaculate perfection in Mary.

Such is her prerogative of sinless perfection, and it is, as her maternity, for the sake of Emmanuel. Hence she answered the angel's salutation, "full of grace" (Lk 1:28), with the humble acknowledgement, "Behold, I am the handmaid of the Lord" (Lk 1:38). And like to this is her third prerogative, which follows both from her maternity and from her purity: her intercessory power. For, if "God does not listen to sinners, but if any one is a worshiper of God and does his will, God listens to him" (Jn 9:31); if faithful Abraham was required to pray for Abimelech (Gn 20:17); if patient Job was to pray for his friends (Job 42:10); if meek Moses, by lifting up his hands, turned the battle in favor of Israel against Amalec (Ex 17:11): why should we wonder at hearing that Mary, the only spotless child of Adam's seed, has a transcendent influence with the God of grace? And if the Gentiles at Jerusalem sought Philip, because he was an apostle, when they desired access to Jesus, and Philip spoke to Andrew, as still more closely in our Lord's confidence, and then both came to him (Jn 12:22), is it strange that the mother should have power with the Son, distinct in kind from that of the purest angel and the most triumphant saint? If we have faith to admit the Incarnation itself, we must admit it in its fulness. Why then should we be startled by the gracious appointments which arise out of it, or are necessary to it, or are included in it? If the Creator comes on earth in the form of a servant and a creature, why may not his mother rise to be the Queen of heaven and be clothed with the sun and have the moon under her feet?

December 9

St. Juan Diego

Divine Calls

It would be well if we understood this great truth: that Christ is, as it were, walking among us, and by his hand, or eye, or voice, bidding us follow him. We do not understand that his call is a thing which takes place now. We think it took place in the apostles' days, but we do not believe in it; we do not look out for it in our own case. We have not eyes to see the Lord.

Now what I mean is this: that they who are living religiously have from time to time truths they did not know before, or had no need to consider, brought before them forcibly, truths which involve duties, which are in fact precepts and claim obedience. In this and such-like ways Christ calls us now. There is nothing miraculous or extraordinary in his dealings with us. He works through our natural faculties and circumstances of life. Still what happens to us in Providence is in all essential respects what his voice was to those whom he addressed when on earth. Whether he commands by a visible presence, or by a voice, or by our consciences, it matters not, so long as we feel it to be a command. If it is a command, it may be obeyed or disobeyed. It may be accepted as Samuel or St. Paul accepted it, or put aside after the manner of the young man who had great possessions.

These divine calls are now commonly, from the nature of the case, sudden, and as indefinite and obscure in their consequences as in former times. The accidents and events of life are, as is obvious, one special way in which the calls I speak of come to us; and they, as we all know, are in their very nature, and as the word *accident* implies, sudden and unexpected. A man is going on as usual; he comes home one day and finds a letter or a message or a person whereby a sudden trial comes on him, which, if met religiously, will be the means of advancing him to a higher state of religious excellence, which at present he as little comprehends as the unspeakable words heard by St. Paul in paradise.

By a trial we commonly mean something which if encountered well will confirm a man in his present way. But I am speaking of something more than this: of what will not only confirm him, but raise him into a high state of knowledge and holiness.

Many persons will find it very striking on looking back at their past lives to observe what different notions they entertained at different periods of what divine truth was, what was the way of pleasing God, and what things were allowable or not, what excellence was, and what happiness. It may so happen that we find ourselves, how or why we cannot tell, much more able to obey God in certain respects than heretofore. Our minds are so strangely constituted, it is impossible to say whether it is from the growth of habit suddenly showing itself, or from an unusual gift of divine grace poured into our hearts, but so it is. Let our temptation be to sloth, or irresolution, or worldly anxiety, or pride, or to other more base and miserable sins: we may suddenly find ourselves possessed of a power of self-command which we had not before. Or again, we may have a resolution grow on us to serve God more strictly than heretofore. This is a call to higher things. Let us beware lest we receive the grace of God in vain. Let us beware of lapsing back. Let us avoid temptation. Let us strive by quietness and caution to cherish the feeble flame and shelter it from the storms of the world. God may be bringing us into a higher world of religious truth: let us work with him.

Nothing is more certain in matter of fact than that some men do feel themselves called to high duties and works to which others are not called. Why this is we do not know. Whether it be that those who are not called forfeit the call from having failed in former trials, or have been called and have not followed, or that though God gives baptismal grace to all, yet he really does call some men by his free grace to higher things than others, but so it is: this man sees sights which that man does not see, has a larger faith, a more ardent love, and a more spiritual understanding.

No one has any leave to take another's lower standard of holiness for his own. It is nothing to us what others are. If God calls us to greater renunciation of the world, and exacts a sacrifice of our hopes and fears, this is our gain, this is a mark of his love for us, this is a thing to be rejoiced in. Such thoughts, when properly entertained, have no tendency to puff us up, for if the prospect is noble, yet the risk is more fearful. While we pursue high excellence, we walk among precipices, and a fall is easy. Hence the apostle says, "Work out your own salvation with fear and trembling; for God is at work in you" (Phil 2:12-13).

Again, the more men aim at high things, the more sensitive perception they have of their own shortcomings, and this again is adapted to humble them especially. We need not fear spiritual pride, then, in following Christ's call, if we follow it in earnest. Earnestness has no time to compare itself with the state of others; earnestness has too vivid a feeling of its own infirmities to be elated at itself. Earnestness is simply set on doing God's will. It simply says, "Speak, for your servant hears" (1 Sm 3:10). Oh, that we had more of this spirit! Oh, that we could take that simple view of things as to feel that the one thing which lies before us is to please God! What gain is it to please the world, to please the great, nay, even to please those whom we love, compared with this? What gain is it to be applauded, admired, courted, followed, compared with this one aim of not being disobedient to a heavenly vision? What can this world offer comparable with that insight into spiritual things, that keen faith, that heavenly peace, that high sanctity, that everlasting righteousness, that hope of glory, which they have who in sincerity love and follow our Lord Jesus Christ?

Let us beg and pray him day by day to reveal himself to our souls more fully, to quicken our senses, to give us sight and hearing, taste and touch of the world to come, so to work within us that we may sincerely say, "You guide me with your counsel, and afterward you will receive me to glory. Whom have I in heaven but you? And there is nothing upon earth that I desire besides you. My flesh and my heart may fail, but God is the strength of my heart and my portion forever" (Ps 73:24-26).

December 10

Shrinking from Christ's Coming

Before Christ came, the faithful remnant of Israel were consoled with the promise that their eyes should see him who was to be their salvation. "For you who fear my name the sun of righteousness shall rise, with healing in its wings" (Mal 4:2). Yet it is observable that the prophecy, though cheering and encouraging, had with it something of an awful character too. First, it was said, "The Lord whom you seek will suddenly come to his temple; the messenger of the covenant in whom you delight." Yet it is soon added, "But who can endure the day of his coming, and who can stand when he appears? For he is like a refiner's fire and like fullers' soap" (Mal 3:1-2).

We too are looking out for Christ's coming. We are bid to look out; we are bid to pray for it. And yet it is to be a time of judgment. It is to be the deliverance of all saints from sin and sorrow forever. Yet they, every one of them, must undergo an awful trial. How then can any look forward to it with joy, not knowing (for no one knows) the certainty of his own salvation? And the difficulty is increased when we come to pray for it, to pray for its coming soon: how can we pray that Christ would come, that the day of judgment would hasten, that his kingdom would come, that his kingdom may be at once, when by so coming he would be shortening the time of our present life and cut off those precious years given us for conversion, amendment, repentance, and sanctification? Is there not an inconsistency in professing to wish our judge already come when we do not feel ourselves ready for him? In what sense can we really and heartily pray that he would cut short the time, when our conscience tells us that, even were our life longest, we should have much to do in a few years?

You ask how you can make up your mind to stand before your Lord and God. I ask in turn, how do you bring yourself to come before him now day by day? For what is this but meeting him? Consider what it is you mean by praying, and you will see that at the very time you are asking for the coming of his kingdom you are anticipating that coming and accomplishing the thing you fear. When you pray, you come into his presence. Now reflect on these. You seem to say: I am in myself nothing but a sinner, a man of unclean lips and earthly heart. I am not worthy to enter into his presence. I am not worthy of the least of his mercies. I know he is all-holy, yet I come before him. I place myself under his pure and piercing eyes, which look me through and through, and discern every trace and every motion of evil within me. Why do I do so? First of all, for this reason: To whom should I go? What can I do better? Who is there in the whole world that can help me? Who that will care for me, or pity me, or have any kind of thought of me, if I cannot obtain it from him? I know he is of purer eyes than to behold iniquity; but I know again that he is all-merciful, and that he so sincerely desires my salvation that he has died for me. Therefore, though I am in a great strait, I will rather fall into his hands than into those of any creature.

True it is I could find creatures more like myself, imperfect or sinful. It might seem better to betake myself to some of these who have power with God, and to beseech them to interest themselves in me. But no. Somehow I cannot content myself with this. No, terrible as it is, I had rather go to God alone. I have an instinct within me which leads me to rise and go to my Father, to name the name of his well-beloved Son, and having named it, to place myself unreservedly into his hands, saying, "If you, O Lord, should mark iniquities, Lord, who could stand?

But there is forgiveness with you" (Ps 130:3-4). This is the feeling in which we come to confess our sins, and to pray to God for pardon and grace day by day; and, observe, it is the very feeling in which we must prepare to meet him when he comes visibly. Why, even children of this world can meet a judicial process and a violent death with firmness. I do not say that we must have any of their pride or their self-trusting tranquility. And yet there is a certain composure and dignity which become us who are born of immortal seed, when we come before our Father. If indeed we have habitually lived to the world, then truly it is natural we should attempt to fly from him whom we have pierced. Then may we well call on the mountains to fall on us and on the hills to cover us. But if we have lived, however imperfectly, yet habitually, in his fear, if we trust that his Spirit is in us, then we need not be ashamed before him. We shall then come before him, as now we come to pray: with profound abasement, with awe, with self-renunciation, still as relying upon the Spirit which he has given us, with our faculties about us, with a collected and determined mind, and with hope. He who cannot pray for Christ's coming ought not in consistency to pray at all.

I have spoken of coming to God in prayer generally; but if this is awful, much more is coming to him in the sacrament of Holy Communion, for this is in very form an anticipation of his coming, a near presence of him in earnest of it. They indeed who are in the religious practice of communicating understand well enough how it is possible to feel afraid and yet to come. Surely it is possible, and the case is the same as regards the future day of Christ. You must tremble, and yet pray for it. We have all of us experienced enough even of this life to know that the same seasons are often most joyful and also most painful. Instances of this must suggest themselves to all men. Consider the loss of friends, and say whether joy and grief, triumph and humiliation, are not strangely mingled, yet both really preserved. The joy does not change the grief, nor the grief the joy, into some third feeling: they are incommunicable with each other. Both remain; both affect us. Or consider the mingled feelings with which a son obtains forgiveness of a father: the soothing thought that all displeasure is at an end, the veneration, the love, and all the indescribable emotions, most pleasurable, which cannot be put into word, with still his bitterness against himself. Such is the temper in which we desire to come to the Lord's table; such in which we must pray for his coming; such in which his elect will stand before him when he comes.

December 11

Unreal Words

Nothing is so rare as honesty and singleness of mind, so much so, that a person who is really honest is already perfect. Insincerity was an evil which sprang up within the Church from the first. Ananias and Simon were not open foes of the apostles, but false brethren. And, as foreseeing what was to be, our Savior is remarkable in his ministry for nothing more than the earnestness of the arguments which he addressed to those who came to him against taking up religion lightly, or making promises which they were likely to break.

To make professions is to play with edged tools unless we attend to what we are saying. Words have a meaning, whether we mean that meaning or not; and they are imputed to us in their real meaning, when our not meaning it is our own fault. He who takes God's name in vain is not counted guiltless because he means nothing by it. He cannot frame a language for himself. And they who make professions, of whatever kind, are heard in the sense of those professions, and are not excused because they themselves attach no sense to them. "By your words you will be justified, and by your words you will be condemned" (Mt 12:37).

It is very common in all matters, not only in religion, to speak in an unreal way, that is, when we speak on a subject with which our minds are not familiar. If you were to hear a person who knew nothing about military matters giving directions how soldiers on service should conduct themselves, or how their food and lodging, or their marching, was to be duly arranged, you would be sure that his mistakes would be such as to excite the ridicule and contempt of men experienced in warfare.

Again, persons who have not attended to the subject of morals, or to politics, or to matters ecclesiastical, or to theology, do not know the relative value of questions which they meet with in these departments of knowledge. They do not understand the difference between one point and another. The one and the other are the same to them. They look at them as infants gaze at the objects which meet their eyes, in a vague unapprehensive way, as if not knowing whether a thing is a hundred miles off or close at hand, whether great or small, hard or soft. They have no means of judging, no standard to measure by, and they give judgment at random, saying yea or nay on very deep questions, according as their fancy is struck at the moment, or as some clever or specious argument happens to come across them. Consequently they are inconsistent, say one thing one day, another the next, and if they must act, act in the dark. All this is to be unreal.

It takes a long time really to feel and understand things as they are. We learn to do so only gradually. Profession beyond our feelings is only a fault when we may help it, when either we speak when we need not speak, or do not feel when we might have felt. Hard insensible hearts, ready and thoughtless talkers, these are they whose unreality is a sin. It is the sin of every one of us, in proportion as our hearts are cold or our tongues excessive.

But the mere fact of our saying more than we feel is not necessarily sinful. St. Peter did not rise up to the full meaning of his confession, "You are the Christ" (Mt 16:16), yet he was pronounced blessed. St. James and St. John said "We are able" (Mt 20:22) without clear apprehension, yet without offense. We ever promise things greater than we master, and we wait on God to enable us to perform them. Our promising involves a prayer for light and strength.

Be in earnest, and you will speak of religion where, and when, and how you should. Aim at things, and your words will be right without aiming. There are ten thousand ways of looking at this world, but only one right way. The man of pleasure has his way, the man of gain his, and the man of intellect his. Poor men and rich men, governors and governed, prosperous and discontented, learned and unlearned, each has his own way of looking at the things which come before him, and each has a wrong way. There is but one right way: it is the way in which God looks at the world. Aim at looking at it in God's way. Aim at seeing things as God sees them. Aim at forming judgments about persons, events, ranks, fortunes, changes, objects, such as God forms. Aim at looking at this life as God looks at it. Aim at looking at the life to come, and the world unseen, as God does. All things that we see are but shadows to us and delusions unless we enter into what they really mean.

It is not an easy thing to learn that new language which Christ has brought us. He has interpreted all things for us in a new way; he has brought us a religion which sheds a new light on all that happens. Try to learn this language. Do not get it by rote, or speak it as a thing of course. Try to understand what you say. Time is short, eternity is long; God is great, man is weak; he stands between heaven and hell; Christ is his Savior; Christ has suffered for him. The Holy Spirit sanctifies him; repentance purifies him, faith justifies, works save. These are solemn truths, which need not be actually spoken, except in the way of creed or of teaching, but which must be laid up in the heart. That a thing is true is no reason that it should be said, but that it should be done, that it should be acted upon, that it should be made our own inwardly.

Let us guard against frivolity, love of display, love of being talked about, love of singularity, love of seeming original. Let us aim at meaning what we say, and saying what we mean. Let us aim at knowing when we understand a truth, and when we do not. When we do not, let us take it on faith, and let us profess to do so. Let us receive the truth in reverence, and pray God to give us a good will, and divine light, and spiritual strength, that it may bear fruit within us.

December 12

Our Lady of Guadalupe

On the Fitness of the Glories of Mary

Blessed Mary has no chance place in the divine dispensation. The Word of God did not merely come to her and go from her. He did not pass through her, as he visits us in Holy Communion. It was no heavenly body which the Eternal Son assumed, fashioned by the angels and brought down to this lower world. No, he imbibed, he absorbed into his Divine Person her blood and the substance of her flesh; by becoming man of her, he received her lineaments and features, as the appropriate character in which he was to manifest himself to mankind. The child is like the parent, and we may well suppose that by his likeness to her was manifested her relationship to him. Her sanctity comes, not only of her being his mother, but also of his being her son. "If the dough offered as first fruits is holy," says St. Paul, "so is the whole lump; and if the root is holy, so are the branches" (Rom 11:16). And hence the titles which we are accustomed to give to her. He is the Wisdom of God; she therefore is the Seat of Wisdom. His presence is heaven; she therefore is the Gate of Heaven. He is infinite mercy; she then is the Mother of Mercy. She is the Mother of "fair love, and of fear, and of knowledge, and of holy hope" (Sir 24:24 DR). Is it wonderful then that she has left behind her in the Church below an odor like cinnamon and balm, and sweetness like choice myrrh? (cf. Sir 24:20 DR).

Such, then, is the truth ever cherished in the deep heart of the Church, and witnessed by the keen apprehension of her children, that no limits but those proper to a creature can be assigned to the sanctity of Mary. Did Abraham believe that a son should be born to him of his aged wife? Then Mary's faith must be held greater when she accepted Gabriel's message. Did Judith consecrate her widowhood to God to the surprise of her people? Much more did Mary, from her first youth, devote her virginity. Did Samuel, when a child, inhabit the Temple, secluded from the world? Mary too was by her parents lodged in the same holy precincts, even at the age when children first can choose between good and evil. St. John the Baptist was sanctified by the Spirit before his birth; shall Mary be only equal to him? Is it not fitting that her privilege should surpass his? Is it wonderful, if grace, which anticipated his birth by three months, should in her case run up to the very first moment of her being, outstrip the imputation of sin, and be beforehand with the usurpation of Satan? Mary must surpass all the saints; the very fact that certain privileges are known to have been theirs persuades us, almost from the necessity of the case, that she had the same and higher. Her conception was immaculate, in order that she might surpass all saints in the date as well as the fulness of her sanctification.

If the Mother of Emmanuel ought to be the first of creatures in sanctity and in beauty; if it became her to be free of all sin from the very first, and from the moment she received her first grace to begin to merit more; and if such as was her beginning, such was her end, her conception immaculate and her death an assumption; if she died, but revived, and is exalted on high: what is befitting in the children of such a mother, but an imitation, in their measure, of her devotion, her meekness, her simplicity, her modesty, and her sweetness? Her glories are not only for the sake of her Son, they are for our sakes also. Let us copy her faith, who received God's message by the angel without a doubt; her patience, who endured St. Joseph's surprise without a word; her obedience, who went up to Bethlehem in the winter and bore our Lord in a stable; her meditative spirit, who pondered in her heart what she saw and heard about him; her fortitude, whose heart the sword went through; her self-surrender, who gave him up during his ministry and consented to his death.

Above all, let us imitate her purity, who, rather than relinquish her virginity, was willing to lose him for a Son. What need have we of the intercession of the Virgin-mother, of her help, of her pattern, in this respect! What shall bring us forward in the narrow way, if we live in the world, but the thought and patronage of Mary? What shall seal our senses, what shall tranquilize our heart, when sights and sounds of danger are around us, but Mary? What shall give us patience and endurance, when we are wearied out with the length of the conflict with evil, with the unceasing necessity of precautions, with the irksomeness of observing them, with the tediousness of their repetition, with the strain upon the mind, with our forlorn and cheerless condition, but a loving communion with her! She will comfort us in our discouragements, solace us in our fatigues, raise us after our falls, reward us for our successes. She will show us her Son, our God and our all. When our spirit is excited, or relaxed, or depressed, when it loses its balance, when it is restless and wayward, when it is sick of what it has, and hankers after what it has not, when our eye is solicited with evil and our mortal frame trembles under the shadow of the tempter, what will bring us to ourself, to peace and to health, but the cool breath of the Immaculate and the fragrance of the Rose of Sharon? It is the boast of the Catholic religion, that it has the gift of making the heart chaste; and why is this, but that it gives us Jesus Christ for our food, and Mary for our nursing mother? Go to her for the royal heart of innocence. She is the beautiful gift of God, which outshines the fascinations of a bad world, and which no one ever sought in sincerity and was disappointed. She is the personal type and representative image of that spiritual life and renovation in grace without which no one shall see God.

December 13
St. Lucy

Watching

Our Savior gave this warning when he was leaving this world, leaving it, that is, as far as his visible presence is concerned. He looked forward to the many hundred years which were to pass before he came again. He foresaw the state of the world and the Church, as we see it this day, when his prolonged absence has made it practically thought that he never will come back in visible presence, and he mercifully whispers into our ears, not to trust in what we see, not to share in that general unbelief, not to be carried away by the world, but to "take heed, watch, and pray" (Mk 13:33), and look out for his coming.

Let us then consider this most serious question, which concerns every one of us so nearly: what is it to watch for Christ?

He watches for Christ who has a sensitive, eager, apprehensive mind; who is awake, alive, quick-sighted, zealous in seeking and honoring him; who looks out for him in all that happens, and who would not be surprised, who would not be over-agitated or overwhelmed, if he found that he was coming at once.

And he watches with Christ, who, while he looks on to the future, looks back on the past, and does not so contemplate what his Savior has purchased for him, as to forget what he has suffered for him. He watches with Christ, whoever commemorates and renews in his own person Christ's cross and agony, and gladly takes up that mantle of affliction which Christ wore here, and left behind him when he ascended. And hence in the epistles, often as the inspired writers show their desire for his second coming, as often do they show their memory of his first, and never lose sight of his crucifixion in his resurrection. Thus if St. Paul reminds the Romans that they wait for "the redemption of our bodies" (Rom 8:23) at the Last Day, he also says, "provided we suffer with him in order that we may also be glorified with him" (Rom 8:17). If he speaks to the Corinthians of waiting for "the revealing of our Lord Jesus Christ" (1 Cor 1:7), he also speaks of "always carrying in the body the death of Jesus, so that the life of Jesus may also be made manifested in our bodies" (2 Cor 4:10). If to the Philippians of "the power of his resurrection," he adds at once his prayer that he "may share his sufferings, becoming like him in his death" (Phil 3:10). If he consoles the Colossians with the hope that "when Christ who is our life appears, then you also will appear with him in glory" (Col 3:4), he has already declared that he is completing "what is lacking in Christ's afflictions for the sake of his body, that is, the Church" (Col 1:24). Thus, the thought of what Christ is must not obliterate from the mind the thought of what he was; and faith is always sorrowing with him while it rejoices. And the same union of opposite thoughts is impressed on us in Holy Communion, in which we see Christ's death and resurrection together, at one and the same time; we commemorate the one, we rejoice in the other. We make an offering, and we gain a blessing.

This then is to watch: to be detached from what is present, and to live in what is unseen; to live in the thought of Christ as he came once, and as he will come again; to desire his second coming, from our affectionate and grateful remembrance of his first. And this it is, in which we shall find that men in general are wanting. They are indeed without faith and love also, but at least they profess to have these graces, nor is it easy to convince them that they have not. For they consider they have faith, if they do but own that the Bible came from God, or that they trust wholly in Christ for salvation; and they consider they have love if they obey some of the most obvious of God's commandments. Love and faith they think they have; but surely they do not even fancy that they watch. What is meant by watching, and how it is a duty, they have no definite idea; and thus it accidentally happens that watching is a suitable test of a Christian, in that it is that particular property of faith and love, which is the life or energy of faith and love, the way in which faith and love, if genuine, show themselves.

Year passes after year silently. Christ's coming is ever nearer than it was. O that, as he comes nearer earth, we may approach nearer heaven! O, my brethren, pray him to give you the heart to seek him in sincerity. Pray him to make you in earnest. You have one work only, to bear your cross after him. Resolve in his strength to do so. Resolve to be no longer beguiled by shadows of religion, or by words, or by disputings, or by notions, or by high professions, or by excuses, or by the world's promises or threats. Pray him to give you what Scripture calls "an honest and good heart" (Lk 8:15) or "a whole heart" (1 Chr 29:9), and, without waiting, begin at once to obey him with the best heart you have. Any obedience is better than none; any profession which is disjoined from obedience is a mere pretense and deceit. Any religion which does not bring you nearer to God is of the world. You have to seek his face; obedience is the only way of seeking him. All your duties are obediences. If you are to believe the truths he has revealed, to regulate yourselves by his precepts, to be frequent in his ordinances, to adhere to his Church and people, why is it, except because he has bid you? And to do what he bids is to obey him, and to obey him is to approach him. Every act of obedience is an approach, an approach to him who is not far off, though he seems so, but close behind this visible screen of things which hides him from us. He is behind this material framework; earth and sky are but a veil going between him and us. The day will come when he will rend that veil, and show himself to us. And then, according as we have waited for him, will he recompense us. If we have forgotten him, he will not know us, but "blessed are those servants whom the master finds awake when he comes...he will put on his apron and have them sit at table, and he will come and serve them. If he comes in the second watch, or in the third, and finds them so, blessed are those servants!" (Lk 12:37-38). May this be the portion of every one of us! It is hard to attain it, but it is woeful to fail. Life is short. Death is certain. The world to come is everlasting.

December 14
St. John of the Cross

Dispositions for Faith

What is the main guide of the soul, given to the whole race of Adam, outside the true fold of Christ as well as within it, given from the first dawn of reason, given to it in spite of that grievous penalty of ignorance which is one of the chief miseries of our fallen state? It is the light of conscience, "the true light," which "enlightens every man" (Jn 1:9). Whether a man be born in pagan darkness, or in some corruption of revealed religion; whether he has heard the name of the Savior of the world or not; whether he be the slave of some superstition or is in possession of some portions of Scripture and treats the inspired word as a sort of philosophical book which he interprets for himself: in any case, he has within his breast a certain commanding dictate—not a mere sentiment, not a mere opinion, or impression, or view of things, but a law, an authoritative voice—bidding him do certain things and avoid others. I do not say that its particular injunctions are always clear, or that they are always consistent with each other. But what I am insisting on here is this: that it commands, that it praises, it blames, it promises, it threatens, it implies a future, and it witnesses the unseen. It is more than a man's own self. The man himself has not power over it, or only with extreme difficulty. He did not make it. He cannot destroy it. He may silence it in particular cases or directions, he may distort its enunciations, but he cannot emancipate himself from it. He can disobey it. He may refuse to use it, but it remains.

This is conscience, and, from the nature of the case, its very existence carries on our minds to a Being exterior to ourselves.

For else whence did it come? And to a Being superior to ourselves, else whence its strange, troublesome peremptoriness? I say, without going on to the question what it says, and whether its particular dictates are always as clear and consistent as they might be, its very existence throws us out of ourselves, and beyond ourselves, to go and seek for him in the height and depth, whose voice it is. As the sunshine implies that the sun is in the heavens, though we may see it not, as a knocking at our doors at night implies the presence of one outside in the dark who asks for admittance, so this word within us, not only instructs us up to a certain point, but necessarily raises our minds to the idea of a teacher, an unseen teacher. And in proportion as we listen to that word, and use it, not only do we learn more from it, not only do its dictates become clearer, and its lessons broader, and its principles more consistent, but its very tone is louder and more authoritative and constraining. Thus it is, that to those who use what they have, more is given, for, beginning with obedience, they go on to the intimate perception and belief of one God. His voice within them witnesses to him, and they believe his own witness about himself. They believe in his existence, not because others say it, not in the word of man merely, but with a personal apprehension of its truth.

In spite of all that this voice does for them, it does not do enough, as they most keenly and sorrowfully feel. They find it most difficult to separate what it really says, taken by itself, from what their own passion or pride, self-love or self-will, mingles with it. Many is the time when they cannot tell how much that true inward guide commands, and how much comes from a mere earthly source, so that the gift of conscience raises a desire for what it does not itself fully supply. It inspires in them the idea of authoritative guidance, of a divine law, and the desire of possessing it in its fulness, not in mere fragmentary portions or indirect suggestion. It creates in them a thirst, an impatience, for the knowledge of that unseen Lord, and governor, and judge, who as yet speaks to them only secretly, who whispers in their hearts, who tells them something, but not nearly so much as they wish and as they need. Thus, a religious man, who has not the blessing of the infallible teaching of revelation, is led to look out for it for the very reason that he is religious. He has something, but not all; and if he did not desire more, it would be a proof that he had not used, that he had not profited by, what he had. Hence, he will be on the look-out. Such is the definition of every religious man who has not the knowledge of Christ. He is on the look-out. As the Jewish believers were on the look-out for a Messiah who they knew was to come, so at all times, and under all dispensations, and in all sects, there are those who know there is a truth, who know they do not possess it except in a very low measure, who desire to know more, who know that he alone who has taught them what they know, can teach them more, who hope that he will teach them more, and so are on the look-out for his teaching.

There is another reason why they will be thus waiting and watching for some further knowledge of God's will than they at present possess. It is because the more a person tries to obey his conscience, the more he gets alarmed at himself for obeying it so imperfectly. His sense of duty will become more keen, and his perception of transgression more delicate, and he will understand more and more how many things he has to be forgiven. But next, while he thus grows in self-knowledge, he also understands more and more clearly that the voice of conscience has nothing gentle, nothing of mercy in its tone. It is severe, and even stern. It does not speak of forgiveness, but of punishment. It suggests to him a future judgment; it does not tell him how he can avoid it. Moreover, it does not tell him how he is to get better; he feels himself very sinful at the best; he feels himself in bondage to a tyranny which, alas! he loves too well, even while he hates it. And thus, he is in great anguish and cries out in the apostle's words, "Wretched man that I am! Who will deliver me from this body of death?" (Rom 7:24).

December 15

Obedience to God the Way to Faith in Christ

It would have been strange if the God of nature had said one thing, and the God of grace another, if the truths which our conscience taught us without the information of Scripture were contradicted by that information when obtained. But it is not so. There are not two ways of pleasing God. What conscience suggests, Christ has sanctioned and explained: to love God and our neighbor are the great duties of the Gospel as well as of the Law. He who endeavors to fulfil them by the light of nature is in the way towards, is, as our Lord said, "not far from the kingdom" (Mk 12:34), for to him that has, more shall be given.

It is not in one or two places merely that this same doctrine is declared to us. Indeed, all revelation is grounded on those simple truths which our own consciences teach us in a measure, though a poor measure, even without it. It is one God, and none other but he, who speaks first in our consciences, then in his holy Word. And, lest we should be in any difficulty about the matter, he has most mercifully told us so in Scripture, wherein he refers again and again to the great moral law, as the foundation of the truth, which his apostles and prophets, and last of all his Son, have taught us: "Fear God, and keep his commandments; for this is the whole duty of man" (Eccl 12:13).

Yet though this is so plain, both from our own moral sense and the declarations of Scripture, still for many reasons it is necessary to insist upon it; chiefly, because, it being very hard to keep God's commandments, men would willingly persuade themselves, if they could, that strict obedience is not necessary under the Gospel, and that something else will be taken, for Christ's sake, in place of it. Instead of laboring, under God's grace, to change their wills, to purify their hearts, and so prepare themselves for the kingdom of God, they imagine that in that kingdom they may be saved by something short of this, by their baptism, or by their ceremonial observances (the burnt offerings and sacrifices which the scribe disparages), or by their correct knowledge of the truth, or by their knowledge of their own sinfulness, or by some past act of faith which is to last them during their lives, or by some strong habitual persuasion that they are safe; or, again, by the performance of some one part of their duty, though they neglect the rest, as if God said a thing to us in nature, and Christ unsaid it. And, when men wish a thing, it is not hard to find texts in Scripture which may be ingeniously perverted to suit their purpose. The error then being so common in practice, of believing that Christ came to gain for us easier terms of admittance into heaven than we had before (whereas, in fact, instead of making obedience less strict, he has enabled us to obey God more strictly; and instead of gaining easier terms of admittance, he has gained us altogether our admittance into heaven, which before was closed against us); this error being so common, it may be right to insist on the opposite truth, however obvious, that obedience to God is the way to know and believe in Christ.

Now, first, let us consider how plainly we are taught in Scripture that perfect obedience is the standard of Gospel holiness. By St. Paul: "Do not be conformed to this world, but be transformed by the renewal of your mind, that you may prove what is the will of God, what is good and acceptable and perfect" (Rom 12:2). "Neither circumcision counts for anything nor uncircumcision, but keeping the commandments of God" (1 Cor 7:19). "Whatever is true, whatever is honorable, whatever is just, whatever is pure, whatever is lovely, whatever is gracious, if there is any excellence, if there is anything worthy of praise, think about these things" (Phil 4:8). By St. James: "Whoever keeps the whole law but fails in one point has become guilty of all of it" (Jas 2:10). By St. Peter: "Make every effort to supplement your faith with virtue, and virtue with knowledge, and knowledge with self-control, and self-control with steadfastness, and steadfastness with godliness, and godliness with brotherly affection, and brotherly affection with love" (2 Pt 1:5-7). By St. John: "And by this we may be sure that we know him, if we keep his commandments" (1 Jn 2:3). Lastly, by our Lord himself: "He who has my commandments and keeps them, he it is who loves me; and he who loves me will be loved by my Father, and I will love him and manifest myself to him" (Jn 14:21). And, above all, the following clear declaration in the Sermon on the Mount: "Whoever then relaxes one of the least of these commandments and teaches men so, shall be called least in the kingdom of heaven; but he who does them and teaches them shall be called great in the kingdom of heaven" (Mt 5:19).

These texts, and a multitude of others, show that the Gospel leaves us just where it found us, as regards the necessity of our obedience to God; that Christ has not obeyed instead of us, but that obedience is quite as imperative as if Christ had never come; nay, is pressed upon us with additional sanctions, the difference being, not that he relaxes the strict rule of keeping his commandments, but that he gives us spiritual aids, which we have not except through him, to enable us to keep them. Accordingly, Christ's service is represented in Scripture, not as different from that religious obedience which conscience teaches us naturally, but as the perfection of it. We are told again and again that obedience to God leads on to faith in Christ, that it is the only recognized way to Christ, and that, therefore, to believe in him ordinarily implies that we are living in obedience to God. For instance: "Everyone who has heard and learned from the Father comes to me" (Jn 6:45); "He who does what is true, comes to the light" (Jn 3:21), that is, to Christ; "No one can come to me unless the Father who sent me draws him" (Jn 6:44). On the other hand, "He who hates me, hates my Father also" (Jn 15:23); "If you knew me, you would know my Father also" (Jn 8:19); "Anyone who denies the Son does not have the Father" (1 Jn 2:23); "Anyone who goes ahead and does not abide in the doctrine of Christ does not have God; he who abides in the doctrine has both the Father and the Son" (2 Jn 9).

At all times and under all circumstances, as all parts of the Bible inform us, obedience to the light we possess is the way to gain more light. In the words of Wisdom, in the book of Proverbs, "I love those who love me, and those who seek me diligently find me. I walk in the way of righteousness, in paths of justice" (Prv 8:17, 20). Or, in the still more authoritative words of Christ himself, "He who is faithful in a very little, is faithful also in much" (Lk 16:10), and, "To him who has will more be given" (Mk 4:25).

December 16

Christian Repentance

The very best that can be said of the fallen and redeemed race of Adam is that they confess their fall and condemn themselves for it and try to recover themselves. And this state of mind, which is in fact the only possible religion left to sinners, is represented to us in the parable of the prodigal son, who is described as receiving, then abusing, and then losing God's blessings, suffering from their loss, and brought to himself by the experience of suffering. A poor service indeed to offer, but the best we can offer, to make obedience our second choice when the world deserts us, when that is dead and lost to us wherein we were held!

Let it not be supposed that I think that in the lifetime of each one of us there is some clearly marked date at which we began to seek God, and from which we have served him faithfully. This may be so in the case of this person or that, but it is far from being the rule. We may not so limit the mysterious work of the Holy Spirit. He condescends to plead with us continually, and what he cannot gain from us at one time, he gains at another. Repentance is a work carried on at various times, and but gradually and with many reverses perfected. Or rather, and without any change in the meaning of the word *repentance*, it is a work never complete, never entire, unfinished both in its inherent imperfection, and on account of the fresh occasions which arise for exercising it. We are ever sinning; we must ever be renewing our sorrow and our purpose of obedience, repeating our confessions and our prayers for pardon. No need to look back to the first beginnings of our repentance, should we be able to trace these, as something solitary and peculiar in our religious course. We are ever but beginning. The most perfect Christian is to himself but a beginner, a penitent prodigal, who has squandered God's gifts and comes to him to be tried over again, not as a son, but as a hired servant.

The prodigal son waited not for his father to show signs of mercy. He did not merely approach a space, and then stand as a coward, curiously inquiring, and dreading how his father felt towards him. He made up his mind at once to degradation at the best, perhaps to rejection. He arose and went straight on towards his father, with a collected mind; and though his relenting father saw him from a distance and went out to meet him, still his purpose was that of an instant frank submission. Such must be Christian repentance. First, we must put aside the idea of finding a remedy for our sin; then, though we feel the guilt of it, yet we must set out firmly towards God, not knowing for certain that we shall be forgiven. He, indeed, meets us on our way with the tokens of his favor, and so he bears up human faith, which else would sink under the apprehension of meeting the Most High God. Still, for our repentance to be Christian, there must be in it that generous temper of self-surrender, the acknowledgement that we are unworthy to be called any more his sons, the abstinence from all ambitious hopes of sitting on his right hand or his left, and the willingness to bear the heavy yoke of bond-servants, if he should put it upon us.

This, I say, is Christian repentance. Will it be said, "It is too hard for a beginner"? True, but I have not been describing the case of a beginner. The parable teaches us what the character of the true penitent is, not how we actually at first come to God. The longer we live, the more we may hope to attain this higher kind of repentance, namely, in proportion as we advance in the other graces of the perfect Christian character. The truest kind of repentance as little comes at first, as perfect conformity to any other part of God's law. It is gained by long practice; it will come at length. The dying Christian will fulfil the part of the returning prodigal more exactly than he ever did in his former years. When first we turn to God in the actual history of our lives, our repentance is mixed with all kinds of imperfect views and feelings. Doubtless there is in it something of the true temper of simple submission. But the wish of appeasing God on the one hand, or a hard-hearted insensibility about our sins on the other, mere selfish dread of punishment, or the expectation of a sudden easy pardon, these, and such-like principles, influence us, whatever we may say or may think we feel. It is, indeed, easy enough to have good words put into our mouths, and our feelings roused, and to profess the union of utter self-abandonment and enlightened sense of sin, but to claim is not really to possess these excellent tempers. Really to gain these is a work of time. It is when the Christian has long fought the good fight of faith, and by experience knows how few and how imperfect are his best services, then it is that he is able to acquiesce, and most gladly acquiesces in the statement, that we are accepted by faith only in the merits of our Lord and Savior. When he surveys his life at the close of it, what is there he can trust in? What act of it will stand the scrutiny of the Holy God? Of course, no part of it, so much is plain without saying a word. But further, what part of it even is a sufficient evidence to himself of his own sincerity and faithfulness? This is the point which I urge. How shall he know that he is still in a state of grace after all his sins? Doubtless he may have some humble hope of his acceptance. St. Paul speaks of the testimony of his conscience as consoling him; but his conscience also tells him of numberless actual sins, and numberless omissions of duty; and with the awful prospect of eternity before him, and in the weakness of declining health, how shall he collect himself to appear before God? Thus he is after all, in the very condition of the returning prodigal, and cannot go beyond him, though he has served God ever so long. He can but surrender himself to God, as after all, a worse than unprofitable servant, resigned to God's will, whatever it is, with more or less hope of pardon, as the case may be, doubting not that Christ is the sole meritorious author of all grace, resting simply on him who, "if he will," can make him clean (Mt 8:2), but not without fears about himself, because unable, as he well knows, to read his own heart in that clear unerring way in which God reads it. Under these circumstances, how vain it is to tell him of his own good deeds, and to bid him look back on his past consistent life! This reflection will rarely comfort him, and when it does, it will be the recollection of the instances of God's mercy towards him in former years which will be the chief ground of encouragement in it. No, his true saying is that Christ came to call sinners to repentance (Mt 9:13), that he died for the ungodly (Rom 5:6). He acknowledges and adopts, as far as he can, St. Paul's words, and nothing beyond them. "The saying is sure and worthy of full acceptance, that Christ Jesus came into the world to save sinners. And I am foremost of sinners" (1 Tm 1:15).

December 17

Doing Glory to God in Pursuits of the World, Part I

When persons are convinced that life is short, that it is unequal to any great purpose, that it does not display adequately, or bring to perfection the true Christian, when they feel that the next life is all in all, and that eternity is the only subject that really can claim or can fill their thoughts, then they are apt to undervalue this life altogether and to forget its real importance. They are apt to wish to spend the time of their sojourning here in a positive separation from active and social duties. Yet it should be recollected that the employments of this world, though not themselves heavenly, are, after all, the way to heaven, and are valuable, though not in themselves, yet for that to which they lead. But it is difficult to realize both truths at once, and to connect both truths together: steadily to contemplate the life to come, yet to act in this. Those who meditate are likely to neglect those active duties which are, in fact, incumbent upon them, and to dwell upon the thought of God's glory, till they forget to act to his glory. This state of mind is chided in figure in the words of the holy angels to the apostles, when they say, "Men of Galilee, why do you stand looking into heaven?" (Acts 1:11).

In various ways does the thought of the next world lead men to neglect their duty in this, and whenever it does so, we may be sure that there is something wrong, not in their thinking of the next world, but in their manner of thinking of it. For though the contemplation of God's glory may in certain times allowably interfere with the active employments of life, as in the case of the apostles when our Savior ascended, and though such contemplation is even freely allowed or commanded us at certain times of each day, yet that is not a real and true meditation on Christ, but some counterfeit, which makes us dream away our time, or become habitually indolent, or which withdraws us from our existing duties, or unsettles us.

When a man has been roused to serious resolutions, the chances are that he fails to take up with the one and only narrow way which leads to life. The chances are that "the evil one comes" (Mt 13:19) and persuades him to choose some path short of the true one, easier and pleasanter than it. And this is the kind of course to which he is often seduced: to feel a sort of dislike and contempt for his ordinary worldly business as something beneath him. He knows he must have what Scripture calls a spiritual mind, and he fancies that to have a spiritual mind it is absolutely necessary to renounce all earnestness or activity in his worldly employments, to profess to take no interest in them, to despise the natural and ordinary pleasures of life, violating the customs of society, adopting a melancholy air and a sad tone of voice, and remaining silent and absent when among his natural friends and relatives, as if saying to himself, "I have much higher thoughts than to engage in all these perishing miserable things": acting with constraint and difficulty in the things about him; making efforts to turn things which occur to the purpose of what he considers spiritual reflection; using certain Scripture phrases and expressions; delighting to exchange Scripture sentiments with persons whom he meets of his own way of thinking, and the like. He thinks he lives out of the world, and out of its engagements, if he shuts his eyes and sits down doing nothing. Altogether he looks upon his worldly occupation simply as a burden and a cross, and considers it all gain to be able to throw it off.

Now, a man's worldly occupation may be his cross. And, under circumstances it may be right even to retire from the world. But I am speaking of cases when it is a person's duty to remain in his worldly calling, and when he does remain in it, but when he cherishes dissatisfaction with it: whereas what he ought to feel is this, that while in it he is to glorify God, not out of it, but in it, and by means of it, according to the apostle's direction, "never flag in zeal, be aglow in the Spirit, serve the Lord" (Rom 12:11). The Lord Jesus Christ our Savior is best served, and with the most fervent spirit, when men are not slothful in business, but do their duty in that state of life in which it has pleased God to call them.

Now what leads such a person into this mistake is that he sees that most men who engage cheerfully and diligently in worldly business do so from a worldly spirit, from a low carnal love of the world, and so he thinks it is his duty, on the contrary, not to take a cheerful part in the world's business at all. And it cannot be denied that the greater part of the world is absorbed in the world, so much so that I am almost afraid to speak of the duty of being active in our worldly business, lest I should seem to give countenance to that miserable devotion to the things of time and sense, that love of bustle and management, that desire of gain, and that aiming at influence and importance, which abound on all sides. Bad as it is to be languid and indifferent in our secular duties, and to account this religion, yet it is far worse to be the slaves of this world and to have our hearts in the concerns of this world.

But surely it is possible to serve the Lord yet not be slothful in business, not over devoted to it, but not to retire from it. We may do all things whatever we are about to God's glory. We may do all things heartily, as to the Lord, and not to man, being both active yet meditative.

"Do all to the glory of God," says St. Paul, "whether you eat or drink" (1 Cor 10:31), so that it appears nothing is too slight or trivial to glorify him in. We will suppose, then, a man who has lately had more serious thoughts than he had before and determines to live more religiously. In consequence of the turn his mind has taken, he feels a distaste for his worldly occupation. He now feels he would rather be in some other business, though in itself his present occupation is quite lawful and pleasing to God. The ill-instructed man will at once get impatient and quit it, or, if he does not quit it, at least he will be negligent and indolent in it. But the true penitent will say to himself, "No, if it be an irksome employment, so much the more does it suit me. I deserve no better. I do not deserve to be fed even with husks. I am bound to afflict my soul for my past sins. If I were to go in sackcloth and ashes, if I were to live on bread and water, if I were to wash the feet of the poor day by day, it would not be too great a humiliation, and the only reason I do not is that I have no call that way; it would look ostentatious. Gladly then will I hail an inconvenience which will try me without anyone's knowing it. Far from repining, I will, through God's grace, go cheerfully about what I do not like. I will deny myself. I know that with his help what is in itself painful will thus be pleasant as done towards him. I know well that there is no pain but may be borne comfortably, by the thought of him, and by his grace, and the strong determination of the will; nay, none but may soothe and solace me. Nay, even sufferings and torture have before now been rejoiced in and embraced heartily from the love of Christ."

December 18

Doing Glory to God in Pursuits of the World, Part II

Another reason which will animate the Christian will be a desire of letting his light shine before men. He will aim at winning others by his own diligence and activity. He will say to himself, "My parents" or "my employer shall never say of me, religion has spoiled him. They shall see me more active and alive than before. I will be punctual and attentive and adorn the Gospel of God our Savior. My companions shall never have occasion to laugh at any affectation of religious feeling in me. No. I will affect nothing. In a manly way I will, with God's blessing, do my duty. I will not, as far as I can help, dishonor his service by any strangeness or extravagance of conduct, any unreality of words, but they shall see that the fear of God only makes those who cherish it more respectable in the world's eyes as well as more heavenly-minded. What a blessed return it will be for God's mercies to me, if I, who am like a brand plucked out of the burning, be allowed, through his great mercy, to recommend that Gospel to others which he has revealed to me, and to recommend it, as on the one hand by my strictness in attending God's ordinances, in discountenancing vice and folly, and by a conscientious walk; so, on the other hand, by all that is of good report in social life, by uprightness, honesty, prudence, and straightforwardness, by good temper, good-nature, and brotherly love."

Thankfulness to Almighty God, nay, and the inward life of the Spirit itself, will be additional principles causing the Christian to labor diligently in his calling. He will see God in all things.

He will recollect our Savior's life. Christ was brought up to a humble trade. When he labors in his own, he will think of his Lord in his. He will recollect that Christ went down to Nazareth and was obedient to his parents, that he walked long journeys, that he bore the sun's heat and the storm, and had nowhere to lay his head. Again, he knows that the apostles had various employments in the world before their calling: St. Andrew and St. Peter fishermen, St. Matthew a tax-gatherer, and St. Paul, even after his calling, still a tent-maker. Accordingly, in whatever comes upon him, he will endeavor to discern the countenance of his Savior. He will feel that the true contemplation of that Savior lies in his worldly business; that as Christ is seen in the poor, and in the persecuted, and in children, so is he seen in the employments which he puts upon his chosen, whatever they be; that in attending to his own calling he will be meeting Christ, that while performing it, he will see Christ revealed to his soul amid the ordinary actions of the day.

True humility is another principle which will lead us to desire to glorify God in our worldly employments if possible, instead of resigning them. Christ evidently puts his greater blessings on those whom the world despises. He has bid his followers take the lowest seat. He says that he who would be great must be as the servant of all, that he who humbles himself shall be exalted, and he himself washed his disciples' feet. Nay, he tells us, that he will gird himself and serve them who have watched for him, an astonishing condescension which makes us almost dumb with fear and rejoicing. All this has its effect upon the Christian, and he sets about his business with diligence, and without a moment's delay, delighting to humble himself, and to have the opportunity of putting himself in that condition of life which our Lord especially blessed.

Lastly, we see what judgment to give in a question sometimes agitated, whether one should retire from worldly business at the close of life, to give our thoughts more entirely to God. To wish to do so is natural. A great many persons are not allowed the privilege; a great many are allowed it through increasing infirmities or extreme old age; but everyone, I conceive, if allowed to choose, would think it a privilege to be allowed it. But let us consider what is the reason of this so natural a wish. I fear a great number of persons who aim at retiring from the world's business do so under the notion of their then enjoying themselves somewhat after the manner of the rich man in the Gospel who said "Soul, you have ample goods laid up for many years" (Lk 12:19). If this is the predominant aim of anyone, of course I need not say that it is a fatal sin, for Christ himself has said so. Others there are who are actuated by a mixed feeling; they look to their last years as a time of retirement, in which they may both enjoy themselves and prepare for heaven. And thus they satisfy both their conscience and their love of the world. At present religion is irksome to them; but then, as they hope, duty and pleasure will go together. Now, putting aside all other mistakes which such a frame of mind evidences, let it be observed, that if they are at present not serving God with all their hearts, but look forward to a time when they shall do so, then it is plain that, when at length they do put aside worldly cares and turn to God, if ever they do, that time must necessarily be a time of deep humiliation, if it is to be acceptable to him, not a comfortable retirement. Who ever heard of a pleasurable, easy, joyous repentance? It is a contradiction in terms. These men, if they do but reflect a moment, must confess that their present mode of life, supposing it to be not so strict as it should be, is heaping up tears and groans for their last years, not enjoyment. The longer they live as they do at present, not only the more unlikely is it that they will repent at all, but even if they do, the more bitter, the more painful must their repentance be. The only way to escape suffering for sin hereafter is to suffer for it here. Sorrow here or misery hereafter: they cannot escape one or the other.

Not for any worldly reason, then, does the Christian desire leisure and retirement for his last years. Nay, he will be content to do without these blessings, and the highest Christian of all is he whose heart is so stayed on God that he does not wish or need it, whose heart is so set on things above that things below as little excite, agitate, unsettle, distress, and seduce him, as they stop the course of nature, as they stop the sun and moon, or change summer and winter. Such were the apostles, who went out to all lands, full of business, and yet full too of sweet harmony, even to the ends of the earth. Their calling was heavenly, but their work was earthly; they were in labor and trouble till the last, yet consider how calmly St. Paul and St. Peter write in their last days. St. John, on the other hand, was allowed in a great measure to retire from the cares of his pastoral charge, and such, I say, will be the natural wish of every religious man, whether his ministry be spiritual or secular; for though he may contemplate God as truly and be as holy in heart in active business as in quiet, still it is more becoming and suitable to meet the stroke of death (if it be allowed us) silently, collectedly, solemnly, than in a crowd and a tumult. And hence it is, among other reasons, that we pray to be delivered from sudden death.

On the whole, then, what I have said comes to this, that whereas Adam was sentenced to labor as a punishment, Christ has by his coming sanctified it as a means of grace and a sacrifice of thanksgiving, a sacrifice cheerfully to be offered up to the Father in his name.

December 19

Feasting in Captivity

When we reflect upon the present state of the Church throughout the world, so different from that which was promised to her in prophecy, the doubt is apt to suggest itself to us whether it is right to rejoice when there is so much to mourn over and to fear. Is it right to keep holiday when the Spouse of Christ is in bondage and the iron almost enters into her soul? We know what prophecy promises us: a holy Church set upon a hill; an imperial Church, far-spreading among the nations, loving truth and peace, binding together all hearts in charity, and uttering the words of God from inspired lips; a kingdom of heaven upon earth that is at unity within itself, peace within its walls and plenteousness within its palaces; a glorious Church, not having spot or wrinkle or any such thing, but holy and without blemish (cf. Eph 5:27). And alas! What do we see? We see the Kingdom of God to all appearances broken into fragments, authority in abeyance, separate portions in insurrection, brother armed against brothers, truth a matter not of faith but of controversy. And looking at our own portion of the heavenly heritage, we see error stalking abroad in the light of day and over the length of the land unrebuked, nay, invading high places, while the maintainers of Christian truth are afraid to speak, lest it should offend those to whom it is a duty to defer. We see discipline utterly thrown down, the sacraments and ordinances of grace open to those who cannot come without profaning them and getting harm from them. Works of penance almost unthought of, the world and the Church mixed together, and those who discern and mourn over all this looked upon with aversion, because they will not prophesy smooth things and speak peace where there is no peace.

On us have fallen the times described by the Psalmist when he laments "You have breached all his walls; you have laid his strongholds in ruins. All that pass by despoil him; he has become the scorn of his neighbors" (Ps 89:40-41). The days of age have come on us, "the evil days...when you shall say, I have no pleasure in them" (Eccl 12:1), the days when the Bridegroom has been taken away, and when men should fast. How then in the day of our fast can we find pleasure and keep festival?

When men discern duly the forlorn state in which the Spouse of Christ at present lies, how can they have the heart to rejoice? "The ark and Israel and Judah dwell in booths," said Uriah, "and the servants of my lord are camping in the open field; shall I then go to my house, to eat and to drink?...as you live, and as your soul lives, I will not do this thing" (2 Sm 11:11). The desponding soul falls back when it makes the effort; it is not equal to the ceremonial which comes natural to light hearts, and at best but coldly obeys what they anticipate without being bidden. What is to be done with this dull, dispirited, wearied, forlorn, foreboding heart of ours? "By the waters of Babylon, there we sat down and wept, when we remembered Zion. On the willows there we hung up our lyres. For there our captors required of us songs, and our tormentors, mirth, saying, 'Sing us one of the songs of Zion!' How shall we sing the Lord's song in a foreign land?" (Ps 137:1-4).

This must be ever kept in mind, when such thoughts arise within us, that cheerfulness and lightness of heart are not only privileges, but duties. Cheerfulness is a great Christian duty. Whatever be our circumstances, within or without, though "fighting without and fear within" (2 Cor 7:5), yet the apostle's words are express, "Rejoice in the Lord always" (Phil 4:4).

That sorrow, that solicitude, that fear, that repentance, is not Christian which has not its portion of Christian joy, for "God is greater than our hearts" (1 Jn 3:20), and no evil, past or future, within or without, is equal to this saying, that Christ has died and reconciled the world unto himself. We are ever in his presence, be we cast down, or be we exalted, and in his "presence there is fulness of joy" (Ps 16:11). "Let the lowly brother boast in his exaltation, and the rich in his humiliation" (Jas 1:9-10). Whether we eat or drink, or whatever we do, to his glory must we do all, and if to his glory, to our great joy; for his service is perfect freedom, and what are the very angels in heaven but his ministers? Nothing is evil but separation from him; while we are allowed to visit his Temple, we cannot but "enter his gates with thanksgiving, and his courts with praise" (Ps 100:4). "Is anyone," then, "among you suffering? Let him pray. Is any cheerful? Let him sing praise" (Jas 5:13).

Let us recollect this for our own profit, that if it is our ambition to follow the Christians of the first ages, as they followed the apostles, and the apostles followed Christ, they had the discomfort of this world without its compensating gifts. No high cathedrals, no decorated altars, no white-robed priests, no choirs for sacred psalmody, nothing of the order, majesty, and beauty of devotional services had they. But they had trials, afflictions, solitariness, contempt, ill-usage. They were "in toil and hardship, through many a sleepless night, in hunger and thirst, often without food, in cold and exposure" (2 Cor 11:27). If we have only the enjoyment and none of the pain, and they only the pain and none of the enjoyment, in what does our Christianity resemble theirs? What are the tokens of identity between us? Why do we not call theirs one religion and ours another? What points in common are there between the easy religion of this day, and the religion of St. Athanasius, or

St. Chrysostom? How do the two agree, except that the name of Christianity is given to both of them?

O may we be wiser than to be satisfied with an untrue profession and a mere shadow of the Gospel! May God raise our hearts on high to seek first his kingdom and his righteousness, that all other things may be added to us! (cf. Mt 6:33). My brethren, let what is inward be chief with you, and what is outward be subordinate! Think nothing preferable to a knowledge of yourselves, true repentance, a resolve to live to God, to die to the world, deep humility, hatred of sin, and of yourselves as you are sinners, a clear and habitual view of the coming judgment. Let this be first; and secondly, labor for the unity of the Church. Let the peace of Jerusalem and the edification of the body of Christ be an object of prayer, close upon that of your own personal salvation. Pray that a divine influence may touch the hearts of men, and that in spite of themselves, while they wonder at themselves, not to say while others wonder at them, they may confess and preach those Catholic truths which at present they scorn or revile; that so at length the language of the prophecy may be fulfilled to us: "I will return to Zion, and will dwell in the midst of Jerusalem," and "there shall be a sowing of peace; the vine shall yield its fruit, and the ground shall give its increase, and the heavens shall give their dew," and "many peoples and strong nations shall come to seek the LORD of hosts in Jerusalem, and to entreat the favor of the LORD" (Zec 8:3, 12, 22).

December 20

Christian Sympathy

We are all of one nature, because we are sons of Adam; we are all of one nature, because we are brethren of Christ. Our old nature is common to us all, and so is our new nature. And because our old nature is one and the same, therefore is it that our new nature is one and the same. Christ could not have taken the nature of every one of us, unless every one of us had the same nature already. He could not have become our brother, unless we were all brethren already; he could not have made us his brethren, unless by becoming our brother, so that our brotherhood in the first man is the means towards our brotherhood in the second.

I do not mean to limit the benefits of Christ's atoning death, or to dare to say that it may not effect ends infinite in number and extent beyond those expressly recorded. But still so far is plain, that it is by taking our nature that he had done for us what he has done for none else; that, by taking the nature of angels, he would not have done for us what he has done; that it is not only the humiliation of the Son of God, but his humiliation in our nature, which is our life. He might have humbled himself in other natures besides human nature, but it was decreed that the Word should be made flesh. "Since therefore the children share in flesh and blood, he himself likewise partook of the same nature" (Heb 2:14), for "it is not with angels that he is concerned but with the descendants of Abraham" (Heb 2:16).

And since his taking on him our nature is a necessary condition of his imparting to us those great benefits which have accrued to us from his death, therefore, as I have said, it was necessary that we should, one and all, have the same original nature, in order to be redeemed by him. For, in order to be redeemed, we must all have that nature which he the Redeemer took. Had our natures been different, he would have redeemed one and not another. Such a common nature we have, as being one and all children of one man, Adam; and thus the history of our fall is connected with the history of our recovery.

Christ then took our nature, when he would redeem it. He redeemed it by making it suffer in his own person. He purified it, by making it pure in his own person. He first sanctified it in himself, made it righteous, made it acceptable to God, submitted it to an expiatory passion, and then he imparted it to us. He took it, consecrated it, broke it, and said, "Take, and divide it among yourselves."

And moreover, he raised the condition of human nature by submitting it to trial and temptation, that what it failed to do in Adam, it might be able to do in him. Or, in other words, which it becomes us rather to use, he condescended, by an ineffable mercy, to be tried and tempted in it, so that, whereas he was God from everlasting, as the only-begotten of the Father, he took on him the thoughts, affections, and infirmities of man, thereby, through the fulness of his divine nature, to raise those thoughts and affections, and destroy those infirmities, that so, by God's becoming man, men, through brotherhood with him, might in the end become as gods.

There is not a feeling, not a passion, not a wish, not an infirmity, which we have, which did not belong to that manhood which he assumed, except such as is of the nature of sin. There was not a trial or temptation which befalls us, but was, in kind at least, presented before him, except that he had nothing within him, sympathizing with that which came to him from without. He said upon his last and greatest trial,

"The ruler of this world is coming. He has no power over me" (Jn 14:30). Yet at the same time we are mercifully assured that "we have not a high priest who is unable to sympathize with our weaknesses, but one who in every respect has been tempted as we are, yet without sinning" (Heb 4:15). And again, "because he himself has suffered and been tempted, he is able to help those who are tempted" (Heb 2:18).

But what I would today draw attention to is the thought with which I began, namely, the comfort granted to us in being able to contemplate him whom the apostle calls "the man Christ Jesus" (1 Tm 2:5), the Son of God in our flesh. I mean, the thought of him binds us together by a sympathy with one another as much greater than that of mere nature, as Christ is greater than Adam. We were brethren, as being of one nature with him, who was "from the earth, a man of dust"; we are now brethren, as being of one nature with "the man of heaven" (1 Cor 15:47-48). All those common feelings, which we have by birth, are far more intimately common to us now that we have obtained the second birth. Our hopes and fears, likes and dislikes, pleasures and pains, have been molded upon one model, have been wrought into one image, blended and combined unto "the measure of the stature of the fulness of Christ" (Eph 4:13). What they become, who have partaken of "the living bread which came down from heaven" (Jn 6:51), the first converts showed, of whom it is said that they "had all things in common" (Acts 2:44), that "the company of those who believed were of one heart and soul" (Acts 4:32), as having "one body and one Spirit...one hope...one Lord, one faith, one baptism, one God and Father of us all" (Eph 4:4-6). Yes, and one thing needful; one narrow way; one business on earth; one and the same enemy; the same dangers; the same temptations; the same afflictions; the same course of life; the same death; the same resurrection; the same judgment. All these things being the same, and the new nature being the same, and from the Same, no wonder that Christians can sympathize with each other, even as by the power of Christ sympathizing in and with each of them.

This is a consideration full of comfort, but of which commonly we do not avail ourselves as we might. It is one comfortable thought, and the highest of all, that Christ, who is on the right hand of God exalted, has felt all that we feel, sin excepted. But it is very comfortable also, that the new and spiritual man, which he creates in us, or creates us into, that is the Christian, has everywhere the same temptations, and the same feelings under them, whether innocent or sinful; so that, as we are all bound together in our head, so are we bound together, as members of one body, in that body, and believe, obey, sin, and repent, all in common.

December 21

The Church a Home for the Lonely

Did we from our youth up follow the guidings of God's grace, we should, without reasoning and without severe trial, understand that heaven is an object claiming our highest love and most persevering exertions. Such doubtless is the blessedness of some persons; such in a degree is perchance the blessedness of many. There are those who, like Samuel, dwell in the Temple of God holy and undefiled from infancy, and, after the instance of John the Baptist, are sanctified by the Holy Spirit, if not as he, from their mother's womb, yet from their second birth in holy baptism. And there are others who possess this great gift more or less, in whom the divine light has been preserved, even though it has been latent, not quenched or overborne by open sin, even though it has not been from the first duly prized and cherished. Many there are, one would hope, who keep their baptismal robes unstained, even though the wind and storm of this world, and the dust of sloth and carelessness for a while discolor them, till in due season they arouse them from their dreams, and, before it is too late, give their hearts to God. All these, whether they have followed him from infancy, or from childhood, or from boyhood, or from youth, or from opening manhood, have never been wedded to this world; they have never given their hearts to it, or vowed obedience or done folly in things of time and sense. And therefore they are able, from the very power of God's grace, as conveyed to them through the ordinances of the Gospel, to understand that the promise of heaven is the greatest, most blessed promise which could be given.

Others turn from God and fall into courses of willful sin, and they of course lose the divine light originally implanted; and if they are recovered are recovered by a severer discipline. They are recovered by finding disappointment and suffering from that which they had hoped would bring them good; they learn to love God and prize heaven, not by baptismal grace, but by trial of the world. They seek the world, and they are driven by the world back again to God. The world is blessed to them, in God's good providence, as an instrument of his grace transmuted from evil to good, as if a second sacrament, doing over again what was done in infancy, and then undone. They are led to say, with St. Peter, "Lord, to whom shall we go?" (Jn 6:68), for they have tried the world, and it fails them. They have trusted it, and it deceives them. They have leaned upon it, and it pierces them through. They have sought it for indulgence, and it has scourged them for their penance. O blessed lot of those, whose wanderings though they wander are thus overruled, that what they lose of the free gift of God, they regain by his compulsory remedies!

But almost all men, whether they are thereby moved to return to God or not, will on experience feel, and confess, and that in no long time, that the world is not enough for their happiness. And they accordingly seek means to supply their need, though they do not go to religion for it. Though they will not accept God's remedy, yet they confess that a remedy is needed, and have recourse to what they think will prove such. Though they may not love God and his holy heaven, yet they find they cannot take up with the world, or cast their lot with it wholly, much as they may wish it. This leads me to the subject which I propose to consider: the need which mankind lies under of some shelter, refuge, rest, home, or sanctuary from the outward world, and the shelter or secret place which God has provided for them in Christ.

Christ finds us weary of that world in which we are obliged to live and act, whether as willing or unwilling slaves to it. He finds us needing and seeking a home, and making one, as we best may, by means of the creature, since it is all we can do. The world, in which our duties lie, is as waste as the wilderness, as restless and turbulent as the ocean, as inconstant as the wind and weather. It has no substance in it, but is like a shade or phantom; when you pursue it, when you try to grasp it, it escapes from you, or it is malicious and does you a mischief. We need something which the world cannot give; this is what we need, and this it is which the Gospel has supplied.

Our Lord Jesus Christ, after dying for our sins on the cross and ascending on high, left not the world as he found it, but left a blessing behind him. He left in the world what before was not in it: a secret home for faith and love to enjoy, wherever they are found, in spite of the world around us. Do you ask what it is? Scripture speaks of "the foundation of the apostles and prophets, Christ Jesus himself being the cornerstone, in whom the whole structure is joined together and grows into a holy temple in the Lord; in whom you also are built into it for a dwelling place of God in the Spirit" (Eph 2:20-22). This is the Church of God, which is our true home of God's providing, his own heavenly court, where he dwells with saints and angels, into which he introduces us by a new birth, and in which we forget the outward world and its many troubles.

What the visible Temple was to the Jews, such and much more is the kingdom of heaven to us. It is really a refuge and hiding-place, as theirs was, and shuts out the world. When men are distressed with anxiety, care, and disappointment, what do they? They take refuge in their families; they surround themselves with the charities of domestic life and make for themselves an inner world, that their affections may have something to rest on. Such was the gift which inspired men anticipated and we enjoy in the Christian Church. "One thing have I asked of the LORD, that will I seek after; that I may dwell in the house of the

Lord all the days of my life, to behold the beauty of the Lord, and to inquire in his temple. For he will hide me in his shelter in the day of trouble; he will conceal me under the cover of his tent, he will set me high upon a rock" (Ps 27:4-5). There is a great privilege that we may enjoy if we seek it, of dwelling in a heavenly home in the midst of this turbulent world. The world is no helpmeet for man, and a helpmeet he needs. No one, man nor woman, can stand alone: we are so constituted by nature, and the world, instead of helping us, is an open adversary. It but increases our solitariness.

We may be full of sorrows. There may be fightings without and fears within. We may be exposed to the frowns, censure, or contempt of men. We may be shunned by them, or, to take the lightest case, we may be wearied out by the unprofitableness of this world, by its coldness, unfriendliness, distance, and dreariness. We shall need something nearer to us. What is our resource? It is not in arm of man, in flesh and blood, in voice of friend, or in pleasant countenance; it is that holy home which God has given us in his Church. It is that everlasting city in which he has fixed his abode. It is that mount invisible whence angels are looking at us with their piercing eyes and the voices of the dead call us. "He who is in you is greater than he who is in the world" (1 Jn 4:4). "If God is for us, who is against us?" (Rom 8:31).

December 22

Christ Hidden from the World

Of all the thoughts which rise in the mind when contemplating the sojourn of our Lord Jesus Christ upon earth, none perhaps is more affecting and subduing than the obscurity which attended it. I do not mean his obscure condition in the sense of its being humble, but the obscurity in which he was shrouded, and the secrecy which he observed. This characteristic of his first advent is referred to very frequently in Scripture, as in "The light shines in the darkness, and the darkness has not overcome it" (Jn 1:5), and is in contrast with what is foretold about his second advent. Then "every eye will see him" (Rev 1:7), which implies that all shall recognize him. Whereas, when he came for the first time, though many saw him, few indeed discerned him. It had been prophesied, "He had no form or comeliness that we should look at him, and no beauty that we should desire him" (Is 53:2), and at the very end of his ministry, he said to one of his twelve chosen friends, "Have I been with you so long, and yet you do not know me, Philip?" (Jn 14:9).

His condescension in coming down from heaven, in leaving his Father's glory and taking flesh, is so far beyond the power of words or thought that one might consider at first sight that it mattered little whether he came as a prince or a beggar. And yet after all, it is much more wonderful that he came in low estate, for this reason: because it might have been thought beforehand that, though he condescended to come on earth, yet he would not submit to be overlooked and despised. Now, the rich are not despised by the world, and the poor are. If he had come as a great prince or noble, the world without knowing a whit more that he was God, yet would at least have looked up to him and honored him as being a prince. But when he came in low estate, he took upon him one additional humiliation—contempt—being ignored, scorned, rudely passed by, roughly profaned by his creatures.

What were the actual circumstances of his coming? His mother is a poor woman. She comes to Bethlehem to be taxed, traveling, when her choice would have been to remain at home. She finds there is no room in the inn. She is obliged to betake herself to a stable. She brings forth her firstborn Son and lays him in a manger. That little babe, so born, so placed, is none other than the Creator of heaven and earth, the eternal Son of God.

But you may say, how does this concern us? Christ is not here; we cannot in any way insult his majesty. Are we so sure of this? Let it be considered that Christ is still on earth. He said expressly that he would come again. The Holy Spirit's coming is so really his coming, that we might as well say that he was not here in the days of flesh, when he was visibly in the world, as deny that he is here now, when he is here by his divine Spirit. This indeed is a mystery, how God the Son and God the Holy Spirit, two Persons, can be one, how he can be in the Spirit and the Spirit in him, but so it is.

If he is still on earth, yet is not visible (which cannot be denied), it is plain that he keeps himself still in the condition which he chose in the days of his flesh. I mean, he is a hidden Savior, and may be approached (unless we are careful) without due reverence and fear. I say, wherever he is (for that is a further question), still he is here, and again he is secret, and whatever be the tokens of his presence, still they must be of a nature to admit of persons doubting where it is.

When we consider what the tokens of his presence now are, they will be found to be of a nature easily to lead men into irreverence unless they be humble and watchful. For instance, the Church is called his body. What his material body was when he was visible on earth, such is the Church now. It is the instrument of his divine power. It is that which we must approach to gain good from him. It is that which by insulting we awaken his anger. Now, what is the Church but, as it were, a body of humiliation, almost provoking insult and profaneness, when men do not live by faith? An earthen vessel, far more so even than his body of flesh, for that was at least pure from all sin, and the Church is defiled in all her members.

Again, he has made the poor, weak, and afflicted tokens and instruments of his presence, and here again it is plain the same temptation meets us to neglect or profane it. What he was, such are his chosen followers in this world. And as his obscure and defenseless state led men to insult and ill-treat him, so the like peculiarities, in the tokens of his presence, lead men to insult him now. He forewarns us that at the Last Day he will say to the righteous, "I was hungry and you gave me food, I was thirsty and you gave me drink, I was a stranger and you welcomed me, I was naked and you clothed me, I was sick and you visited me, I was in prison and you came to me" (Mt 25:35-36). And he adds, "As you did it to one of the least of these my brethren, you did it to me" (Mt 25:40). In every age, then, Christ is both in the world, and yet not publicly so more than in the days of his flesh.

And a similar remark applies to his ordinances, which are at once most simple, yet most intimately connected with him. St. Paul, in his first epistle to the Corinthians, shows both how easy and how fearful it is to profane the Lord's Supper while he states how great the excess of the Corinthians had been, yet also that it was a failure to discern the Lord's body (1 Cor 11:29). When he was born into the world, the world knew it not. He was laid in a rude manger among the cattle, but "all God's angels" worshipped him (Heb 1:6). Now too he is present upon a table, homely perhaps in make, and dishonored in its circumstances, and faith adores, but the world passes by.

Let us then pray him ever to enlighten the eye of our understanding, that we may belong to the heavenly host, not to this world. As the carnal-minded would not perceive him even in heaven, so the spiritual heart may approach him, possess him, see him, even upon earth.

December 23

The Mystery of Godliness

"The light shines in the darkness, and the darkness has not overcome it" (Jn 1:5). He seemed like other men to the multitude. Though conceived of the Holy Spirit, he was born of a poor woman, who, when guests were numerous, was thrust aside, and gave birth to him in a place for cattle. O wondrous mystery, early manifested, that even in birth he refused the world's welcome! He grew up as a carpenter's son, without education, so that when he began to teach, his neighbors wondered how one who had not learned letters and was bred to a humble craft should become a prophet. He was known as the kinsman and intimate of humble persons; so that the world pointed to them when he declared himself, as if their insufficiency was the refutation of his claims. He was brought up in a town of low repute, so that even the better sort doubted whether good could come out of it. No. He would not be indebted to this world for comfort, aid, or credit, for "the world was made through him, yet the world knew him not" (Jn 1:10). He came to it as a benefactor, not as a guest, not to borrow from it, but to impart to it.

And when he grew up and began to preach the kingdom of heaven, the Holy Jesus took no more from the world then than before. He chose the portion of those saints who preceded and prefigured him: Abraham, Moses, David, Elijah, and his forerunner John the Baptist. He lived at large, without the ties of home or peaceful dwelling; he lived as a pilgrim in the land of promise; he lived in the wilderness. Abraham had lived in tents in the country which his descendants were to enjoy. David had wandered for seven years up and down the same during Saul's persecutions. Moses had been a prisoner in the howling wilderness, all the way from Mount Sinai to the borders of Canaan. Elijah wandered back again from Carmel to Sinai. And the Baptist had remained in the deserts from his youth. Such in like manner was our Lord's manner of life during his ministry. He was now in Galilee, now in Judea. He is found in the mountain, in the wilderness, and in the city; but he chose not to take a home, not even his Almighty Father's Temple at Jerusalem.

Now all this is quite independent of the special objects of mercy which brought him upon earth. Though he had still submitted himself by an incomprehensible condescension to the death on the cross at length, yet why did he from the first so spurn this world, when he was not atoning for its sins? He might at least have had the blessedness of brethren who believed in him. He might have been happy and revered at home. He might have had honor in his own country. He might have submitted but at last to what he chose from the first. He might have delayed his voluntary sufferings till that hour when his Father's and his own will made him the sacrifice for sin.

But he did otherwise, and thus he becomes a lesson to us who are his disciples. He, who was so separate from the world, so present with the Father even in the days of his flesh, calls upon us, his brethren, as we are in him and he in the Father, to show that we really are what we have been made, by renouncing the world while in the world, and living as in the presence of God.

Let them consider this, who think the perfection of our nature still consists, as before the Spirit was given, in the exercise of all its separate functions, animal and mental, not in the subjection and sacrifice of what is inferior in us to what is more excellent. Christ, who is the beginning and pattern of the new creature, lived out of the body while he was in it. His death indeed was required as an expiation; but why was his life so mortified, if such austerity be not man's glory?

Let us at this season approach him with awe and love, in whom resides all perfection, and from whom we are allowed to gain it. Let us come to the Sanctifier to be sanctified. Let us come to him to learn our duty, and to receive grace to do it. At other seasons of the year we are reminded of watching, toiling, struggling, and suffering; but at this season we are reminded simply of God's gifts towards us sinners. "He saved us, not because of deeds done by us in righteousness, but in virtue of his own mercy" (Ti 3:5). We are reminded that we can do nothing, and that God does everything. This is especially the season of grace. We come to see and to experience God's mercies. We come before him as the helpless beings, during his ministry, who were brought on beds and couches for a cure. We come to be made whole. We come as little children to be fed and taught, "like newborn infants" longing for "pure spiritual milk," that by it we may "grow up to salvation" (1 Pt 2:2). This is a time for innocence, and purity, and gentleness, and mildness, and contentment, and peace. It is a time in which the whole Church seems decked in white, in her baptismal robe, in the bright and glistening raiment she wears upon the Holy Mount. Christ comes at other times with garments dyed in blood, but now he comes to us in all serenity and peace, and he bids us rejoice in him and to love one another. This is not a time for gloom, or jealousy, or care, or indulgence, or excess, or license, not for "reveling and drunkenness," not for "debauchery and licentiousness," not for "quarreling and jealousy," as says the apostle (Rom 13:13), but for putting on the Lord Jesus Christ, who "committed no sin," nor was guile "found on his lips" (1 Pt 2:22).

May each Christmas, as it comes, find us more and more like him, who at this time became a little child for our sake, more simple-minded, more humble, more holy, more affectionate, more resigned, more happy, more full of God.

December 24

Equanimity

In other parts of Scripture, the prospect of Christ's coming is made a reason for solemn fear and awe, and a call for watching and prayer, but here a distinct view of the Christian character is set before us, and distinct duties urged on us. "The Lord is at hand," and what then? Why, if so, we must "rejoice in the Lord" (Phil 4:4). We must be conspicuous for "forbearance"; we must "have no anxiety about anything"; we must seek from God's bounty, and not from man, whatever we need; we must abound in "thanksgiving"; and we must cherish, or rather we must pray for, and we shall receive from above, "the peace of God, which passes all understanding," to "keep our hearts and minds in Christ Jesus" (Phil 4:5-7).

Now this is a view of the Christian character definite and complete enough to admit of commenting on, and it may be useful to show that the thought of Christ's coming not only leads to fear, but to a calm and cheerful frame of mind.

Nothing perhaps is more remarkable than that an apostle, a man of toil and blood, a man combating with powers unseen, and a spectacle for men and angels, and much more that St. Paul, a man whose natural temper was so zealous, so severe, and so vehement, I say, nothing is more striking and significant than that St. Paul should have given us this view of what a Christian should be. Here surely is the finger of God; here is the evidence of supernatural influences, making the mind of man independent of circumstances! This is the thought that first suggests itself; and the second is this, how deep and refined is the true Christian spirit! How difficult to enter into, how vast to embrace, how impossible to exhaust! Who would expect such composure and equanimity from the fervent apostle of the Gentiles?

Joy and gladness are also characteristics of him, according to the exhortation in the text, "Rejoice in the Lord always," and this in spite of the fear and awe which the thought of the last day ought to produce in him. It is by means of these strong contrasts that Scripture brings out to us what is the real meaning of its separate portions. If we had been told merely to fear, we should have mistaken a slavish dread, or the gloom of despair, for godly fear; and if we had been told merely to rejoice, we should perhaps have mistaken a rude freedom and familiarity for joy; but when we are told both to fear and to rejoice, we gain thus much at first sight, that our joy is not to be irreverent, nor our fear to be desponding; that though both feelings are to remain, neither is to be what it would be by itself. This is what we gain at once by such contrasts. I do not say that this makes it at all easier to combine the separate duties to which they relate—that is a further and higher work—but this much we gain at once, a better knowledge of those separate duties themselves. And now I am speaking about the duty of rejoicing, and I say, that whatever be the duty of fearing greatly and trembling greatly at the thought of the day of judgment, and of course it is a great duty, yet the command so to do cannot reverse the command to rejoice; it can only so far interfere with it as to explain what is meant by rejoicing. It is as clear a duty to rejoice in the prospect of Christ's coming, as if we were not told to fear it. The duty of fearing does but perfect our joy. That joy alone is true Christian joy, which is informed and quickened by fear, and made thereby sober and reverent.

How joy and fear can be reconciled, words cannot show. Act and deed alone can show how. Let a man try both to fear and to rejoice, as Christ and his apostles tell him, and in time he will learn how; but when he has learned, he will be as little able to explain how it is he does both, as he was before. He will seem inconsistent, and may easily be proved to be so, to the satisfaction of irreligious men, as Scripture is called inconsistent. He becomes the paradox which Scripture enjoins. This is variously fulfilled in the case of men of advanced holiness. They are accused of the most opposite faults: of being proud, and of being mean; of being over-simple, and being crafty; of having too strict, and, at the same time, too lax a conscience; of being unsocial, and yet being worldly; of being too literal in explaining Scripture, and yet of adding to Scripture and superseding Scripture. Men of the world, or men of inferior religiousness, cannot understand them, and are fond of criticizing those who, in seeming to be inconsistent, are but like Scripture teaching.

But to return to the case of joy and fear. It may be objected, that at least those who fall into sin, or who have in times past sinned grievously, cannot have this pleasant and cheerful temper which St. Paul enjoins. I grant it. But what is this but saying that St. Paul enjoins us not to fall into sin? When St. Paul warns us against sadness and heaviness, of course he warns us against those things which make men sad and heavy, and therefore especially against sin, which is an especial enemy of joyfulness. It is not that sorrowing for sin is wrong when we have sinned, but the sinning is wrong which causes the sorrowing. When a person has sinned, he cannot do anything better than sorrow. He ought to sorrow; and so far as he does sorrow, he is certainly not in the perfect Christian state; but it is his sin that has forfeited it. And yet even here sorrow is not inconsistent with rejoicing. For there are few men who are really in earnest in their sorrow, but after a time may be conscious that they are so; and, when man knows himself to be in earnest, he knows that God looks mercifully upon him; and this gives him sufficient reason for rejoicing, even though fear remains. St. Peter could appeal to Christ, "Lord, you know everything; you know that I love you" (Jn 21:17). We, of course, cannot appeal so unreservedly. Still we can timidly appeal. We can say that we humbly trust that, whatever be the measure of our past sins, and whatever of our present self-denial, yet at bottom we do wish and strive to give up the world and to follow Christ. And in proportion as this sense of sincerity is strong upon our minds, in the same degree shall we rejoice in the Lord, even while we fear.

May it be our blessedness, as years go on, to add one grace to another, and advance upward, step by step, neither neglecting the lower after attaining the higher, nor aiming at the higher before attaining the lower. The first grace is faith, the last is love; first comes zeal, afterwards comes loving-kindness; first comes humiliation, then comes peace; first comes diligence, then comes resignation. May we learn to mature all graces in us: fearing and trembling, watching and repenting, because Christ is coming; joyful, thankful, and careless of the future, because he is come.

December 25

The Nativity of the Lord

Religious Joy

There are two principal lessons which we are taught on the great festival which we this day celebrate: lowliness and joy. This surely is a day, of all others, in which is set before us the heavenly excellence and the acceptableness in God's sight of that state which most men have, or may have, allotted to them, humble or private life and cheerfulness in it.

When we think of this day's festival, we are reminded that though this life must ever be a life of toil and effort, yet that, properly speaking, we have not to seek our highest good. It is found, it is brought near us, in the descent of the Son of God from his Father's bosom to this world. It is stored up among us on earth. No longer need men of ardent minds weary themselves in the pursuit of what they fancy may be chief goods; no longer have they to wander about and encounter peril in quest of that unknown blessedness to which their hearts naturally aspire, as they did in heathen times. The text speaks to them and to all: "For to you," it says, "is born this day in the city of David a Savior, who is Christ the Lord" (Lk 2:11).

Nor, again, need we go in quest of any of those things which this vain world calls great and noble. Christ altogether dishonored what the world esteems, when he took on himself a rank and station which the world despises. No lot could be more humble and more ordinary than that which the Son of God chose for himself. So that we have on the feast of the Nativity these two lessons: instead of anxiety within and despondence without, instead of a weary search after great things, to be cheerful and joyful; and, again, to be so in the midst of those obscure and ordinary circumstances of life which the world passes over and thinks scorn of.

Let us consider this in the gracious narrative of which the text (See Lk 2:10-11) is part. What do we read just before the text? That there were certain shepherds keeping watch over their flock by night, and angels appeared to them. Why should the heavenly hosts appear to these shepherds? What was it in them which attracted the attention of the angels and the Lord of angels? Were these shepherds learned, distinguished, or powerful? Were they especially known for piety and gifts? Nothing is said to make us think so. Faith, we may safely say, they had, or some of them, for to him that has more shall be given, but there is nothing to show that they were holier and more enlightened than other good men of the time who waited for the consolation of Israel. Nay, there is no reason to suppose that they were better than the common run of men in their circumstances: simple and fearing God, but without any great advances in piety, or any very formed habits of religion. Why then were they chosen? For their poverty's sake and obscurity. Almighty God looks with a special love, or affection, upon the lowly.

And now comes a second lesson, which I have said may be gained from the festival. The angel honored a humble lot by his very appearing to the shepherds; next he taught it to be joyful by his message. He disclosed good tidings so much above this world as to equalize high and low, rich and poor, one with another. He said, "Be not afraid" (Lk 2:10). This is a mode of address frequent in Scripture, as if man needed some assurance to support him, especially in God's presence. The angel said, "Be not afraid," when he saw the alarm which his presence caused among the shepherds. Even a lesser wonder would have reasonably startled them.

A little religion makes us afraid. When a little light is poured in upon the conscience, there is a darkness visible. The glory of

God alarms while it shines around. His holiness, the range and difficulties of his commandments, the greatness of his power, the faithfulness of his word, frighten the sinner. But religion itself, far from inculcating alarm and terror, says, in the words of the angel, "Be not afraid," for such is his mercy, while Almighty God has poured about us his glory, yet it is a consoling glory, for it is the light of his glory in the face of Jesus Christ. Thus, the heavenly herald tempered the too-dazzling brightness of the Gospel on that first Christmas. The glory of God at first alarmed the shepherds, so he added the good tidings, to work in them a more wholesome and happy temper. Then they rejoiced.

The lesson of joy which the Incarnation gives us is as impressive as the lesson of humility. St. Paul gives us the one lesson in his epistle to the Philippians: "Have this mind among yourselves, which was in Christ Jesus, who, though he was in the form of God, did not count equality with God a thing to be grasped, but emptied himself, taking the form of a servant, being born in the likeness of men" (Phil 2:5-7). And St. Peter gives us the lesson of joyfulness: "Without having seen him you love him; though you do not now see him you believe in him and rejoice with unutterable and exalted joy. As the outcome of your faith you obtain the salvation of your souls" (1 Pt 1:8-9).

Take these thoughts with you to your homes this festive day; let them be with you in your family and social meetings. It is a day of joy. It is good to be joyful; it is wrong to be otherwise. For one day we may put off the burden of our polluted consciences, and rejoice in the perfections of our Savior Christ, without thinking of ourselves, without thinking of our own miserable uncleanness, but contemplating his glory, his righteousness, his purity, his majesty, his overflowing love. We may rejoice in the Lord, and in all his creatures see him. We may enjoy his temporal bounty and partake the pleasant things of earth with him in our thoughts; we may rejoice in our friends for his sake, loving them most especially because he has loved them.

"God has not destined us for wrath, but to obtain salvation through our Lord Jesus Christ, who died for us so that whether we wake or sleep we might live with him" (1 Thes 5:9-10). Let us seek the grace of a cheerful heart, an even temper, sweetness, gentleness, and brightness of mind, as walking in his light, and by his grace. Let us pray him to give us the spirit of ever-abundant, ever-springing love, which overpowers and sweeps away the vexations of life by its own righteousness and strength, and which above all things unites us to him who is the fountain and center of all mercy, loving-kindness, and joy.

December 26

St. Stephen

Martyrdom

St. Stephen, who was one of the seven deacons, is called the protomartyr, as having first suffered death in the cause of the Gospel. Let me take the opportunity of his festival to make some remarks upon martyrdom generally.

The word *martyr* properly means "a witness," but is used to denote exclusively one who has suffered death for the Christian faith. Those who have witnessed for Christ without suffering death are called *confessors*, a title which the early martyrs often made their own, before their last solemn confession unto death, or martyrdom. Our Lord Jesus Christ is the chief and most glorious of martyrs, as "who in his testimony before Pontius Pilate made the good confession" (1 Tm 6:13), but we do not call him a martyr, as being much more than a martyr. True it is, he died for the truth, but that was not the chief purpose of his death. He died to save us sinners from the wrath of God. He was not only a martyr; he was an atoning sacrifice.

He is the supreme object of our love, gratitude, and reverence. Next to him we honor the noble army of martyrs, not indeed comparing them with him "who is God over all, blessed forever" (Rom 9:5), or as if they in suffering had any part in the work of reconciliation, but because they have approached most closely to his pattern of all his servants. They have shed their blood for the Church, fulfilling the text, "He laid down his life for us; and we ought to lay down our lives for the brethren" (1 Jn 3:16). They have followed his steps, and claim our grateful remembrance. Had

St. Stephen shrunk from the trial put upon him, and recanted to save his life, no one can estimate the consequences of such a defection. Perhaps (humanly speaking) the cause of the Gospel would have been lost, the Church might have perished, and, though Christ had died for the world, the world might not have received the knowledge or the benefits of his death. The channels of grace might have been destroyed, the sacraments withdrawn from the feeble and corrupt race which has such need of them.

But in truth, the martyrs of the primitive times were men of very elevated faith, not only our benefactors, but far our superiors. Let us consider what it was then to be a martyr.

First, it was to be a voluntary sufferer. They knew beforehand clearly enough the consequences of preaching the Gospel; they had frequent warnings brought home to them of the sufferings in store for them, if they persevered in their labors of brotherly love. Their Lord and Master had suffered before them; and, besides suffering himself, had expressly foretold their sufferings: "If they persecuted me, they will persecute you" (Jn 15:20). They were repeatedly warned and strictly charged by the chief priests and rulers not to preach in Christ's name. They had experience of lesser punishments from their adversaries in earnest of the greater; and at length they saw their brethren, one by one, slain for persevering in their faithfulness to Christ. Yet they continued to keep the faith, though they might be victims of their obedience any day.

In the next place, the suffering itself of martyrdom was in some respects peculiar. It was a death, cruel in itself, publicly inflicted, and heightened by the fierce exultation of a malevolent populace. When we are in pain, we can lie in peace by ourselves. We receive the sympathy and kind services of those about us, and if we like it, we can retire altogether from the sight of others, and suffer without a witness to interrupt us. But the sufferings of martyrdom were for the most part public, attended with every circumstance of ignominy and popular triumph, as well as with torture. The early Christians had to endure shame after their Master's pattern. They had to die in the midst of enemies who reviled them, and, in mockery, bid them (as in Christ's case) come down from the cross. They were supported on no easy couch, soothed by no attentive friends; and considering how much the depressing power of pain depends on the imagination, this circumstance alone at once separates their sufferings widely from all instances of pain in disease. The unseen God alone was their comforter, and this invests the scene of their suffering with supernatural majesty, and awes us when we think of them.

It is useful to reflect on such subjects in order to humble ourselves. In our struggle against sin, we have "not yet resisted to the point of shedding [our] blood" (Heb 12:4). What are our petty sufferings, which we make so much of, to their pains and sorrows, who lost their friends, and then their own lives for Christ's sake; who were assaulted by all kinds of temptations, the sophistry of Antichrist, the blandishments of the world, the terrors of the sword, the weariness of suspense, and yet fainted not? How far above ours are their afflictions, and their consolations under them! Now I know that such reflections are at once, and with far deeper reason, raised by the thought of the sufferings of Christ himself, but commonly, his transcendent holiness and his depth of woe do not immediately affect us, from their very greatness. We sum them up in a few words, and we speak without understanding. On the other hand, we rise somewhat towards the comprehension of them, when we make use of that heavenly ladder by which his saints have made their way towards him. By contemplating the lowest of his true servants, and seeing how far any one of them surpasses ourselves, we learn to shrink before his ineffable purity, who is infinitely holier than the holiest of his creatures; and to confess ourselves with a sincere mind to be unworthy of the least of all

his mercies. Thus his martyrs lead us to himself, the chief of
martyrs and the king of saints.

May God give us grace to receive these thoughts into our
hearts, and to display the fruit of them in our conduct! What
are we but sinful dust and ashes, grovelers who are creeping
on to heaven, not with any noble sacrifice for Christ's cause,
but without pain, without trouble, in the midst of worldly
blessings! Well, but he can save in the humblest paths of life,
and in the most tranquil times. There is enough for us to do, far
more than we fulfil, in our own ordinary course. Let us strive to
be more humble, faithful, merciful, meek, self-denying than we
are. Let us crucify "the flesh with its passions and desires" (Gal
5:24). This, to be sure, is sorry martyrdom, yet God accepts it
for his Son's sake.

December 27

St. John

Love of Relations and Friends

St. John the apostle and evangelist is chiefly and most familiarly known to us as the disciple "whom Jesus loved" (Jn 13:23). He was one of the three or four who always attended our Blessed Lord, and had the privilege of the most intimate intercourse with him; and, more favored than Peter, James, and Andrew, he was his bosom friend, as we commonly express ourselves. At the solemn supper before Christ suffered, he took his place next him and leaned on his breast. As the other three communicated between the multitude and Christ, so St. John communicated between Christ and them. At that Last Supper, Peter dared not ask Jesus a question himself, but bade John put it to him, who it was that should betray him. Thus St. John was the private and intimate friend of Christ. Again, it was to St. John that our Lord committed his mother, when he was dying on the cross; it was to St. John that he revealed in vision after his departure the fortunes of his Church.

It has been the plan of Divine Providence to ground what is good and true in religion and morals on the basis of our good natural feelings. What we are towards our earthly friends in the instincts and wishes of our infancy, such we are to become at length towards God and man in the extended field of our duties as accountable beings. To honor our parents is the first step towards honoring God; to love our brethren according to the flesh, the first step towards considering all men our brethren. Hence our Lord says, we must become as little children, if we would be saved; we must become in his Church, as men, what we were once in the small circle of our youthful homes.

We know St. John is celebrated for his declarations about Christian love. "Beloved, let us love one another; for love is of God. If we love one another, God abides in us and his love is perfected in us. God is love, and he who abides in love abides in God, and God abides in him" (1 Jn 4:7, 12, 16). Now did he begin with some vast effort at loving on a large scale? Nay, he had the unspeakable privilege of being the friend of Christ. Thus he was taught to love others; first his affection was concentrated, then it was expanded. Next he had the solemn and comfortable charge of tending our Lord's mother, the blessed Virgin, after his departure. Do we not here discern the secret sources of his special love of the brethren? Could he, who first was favored with his Savior's affection, then trusted with a son's office towards his mother, could he be other than a memorial and pattern (as far as man can be) of love—deep, contemplative, fervent, unruffled, unbounded?

The ancients thought so much of friendship that they made it a virtue. In a Christian view, it is not quite this, but it is often accidentally a special test of our virtue. For consider: let us say that this man, and that, not bound by any very necessary tie, find their greatest pleasure in living together; say that this continues for years, and that they love each other's society the more, the longer they enjoy it. Now observe what is implied in this. Young people, indeed, readily love each other, for they are cheerful and innocent, more easily yield to each other, and are full of hope; they are types, as Christ says, of his true converts. But this happiness does not last. Their tastes change. Again, grown persons go on for years as friends, but these do not live together; and, if any accident throws them into familiarity for a while, they find it difficult to restrain their tempers and keep on terms, and discover that they are best friends at a distance. But what is it that can bind two friends together in intimate converse for a course of years, but the participation in something that is unchangeable and essentially good, and what is this but religion? Religious tastes alone are unalterable. The saints of God continue in one way, while the fashions of the world change; and a faithful indestructible friendship may thus be a test of the parties, so loving each other, having the love of God seated deep in their hearts. Not an infallible test certainly, for they may have dispositions remarkably the same, or some engrossing object of this world, literary or other; they may be removed from the temptation to change, or they may have a natural sobriety of temper, which remains contented wherever it finds itself. However, under certain circumstances, it is a lively token of the presence of divine grace in them; and it is always a sort of symbol of it, for there is at first sight something of the nature of virtue in the very notion of constancy, dislike of change being not only the characteristic of a virtuous mind, but in some sense a virtue itself.

And now I have suggested to you a subject of thought for today's festival, and surely a very practical subject, when we consider how large a portion of our duties lies at home. Should God call upon us to preach to the world, surely, we must obey his call; but at present, let us do what lies before us. Little children, let us love one another. Let us be meek and gentle. Let us think before we speak. Let us try to improve our talents in private life. Let us do good, not hoping for a return, and avoiding all display before men. Well may I so exhort you at this season, when we have so lately partaken together the Blessed Sacrament which binds us to mutual love and gives us strength to practice it. Let us not forget the promise we then made, or the grace we then received. We are not our own. We are bought with the blood of Christ. We are consecrated to be temples of the Holy Spirit, an unutterable privilege, which is weighty enough to sink us with shame at our unworthiness, did it not the while strengthen us by the aid itself imparts, to bear its extreme costliness. May we live worthy of our calling, and realize in our own persons the Church's prayers and professions for us.

December 28

The Holy Innocents

The Mind of Little Children

The longer we live in the world, and the further removed we are from the feelings and remembrances of childhood (and especially if removed from the sight of children), the more reason we have to recollect our Lord's impressive action and word, when he called a little child to him, and set him in the midst of his disciples, and said, "Truly, I say to you, unless you turn and become like children, you will never enter the kingdom of heaven. Whoever humbles himself like this child, he is the greatest in the kingdom of heaven" (Mt 18:3-4). And in order to remind us of this our Savior's judgment, the Church, like a careful teacher, calls us back year by year upon this day from the bustle and fever of the world. She takes advantage of the massacre of the Innocents recorded in St. Matthew's Gospel (cf. Mt 2:16-18) to bring before us a truth which else we might think little of, to sober our wishes and hopes of this world, our high ambitious thoughts, or our anxious fears, jealousies, and cares, by the picture of the purity, peace, and contentment which are the characteristics of little children.

If we wish to affect a person, what can we do better than appeal to the memory of times past, and above all to his childhood? Then it was that he came out of the hands of God, with all lessons and thoughts of heaven freshly marked upon him. Who can tell how God makes the soul, or how he new-makes it? We know not. We know that, besides his part in the work, it comes into the world with the taint of sin upon it; and that even regeneration, which removes the curse, does not extirpate the root of evil. Whether it is created in heaven or hell, how Adam's sin is breathed into it, together with the breath of life, and how the Spirit dwells in it, who shall inform us? But this we know full well—we know it from our own recollection of ourselves, and our experience of children—that there is in the infant soul, in the first years of its regenerate state, a discernment of the unseen world in the things that are seen, a realization of what is sovereign and adorable, and an incredulity and ignorance about what is transient and changeable, which mark it as the fit emblem of the matured Christian, when weaned from things temporal, and living in the intimate conviction of the Divine Presence. I do not mean, of course, that a child has any formed principle in his heart, any habits of obedience, any true discrimination between the visible and the unseen, such as God promises to reward for Christ's sake in those who come to years of discretion. Never must we forget that, in spite of his new birth, evil is within him, though in its seed only; but he has this one great gift, that he seems to have lately come from God's presence, and not to understand the language of this visible scene, or how it is a temptation, how it is a veil interposing itself between the soul and God. The simplicity of a child's ways and notions, his ready belief of everything he is told, his artless love, his frank confidence, his confession of helplessness, his ignorance of evil, his inability to conceal his thoughts, his contentment, his prompt forgetfulness of trouble, his admiring without coveting, and, above all, his reverential spirit, looking at all things about him as wonderful, as tokens and types of the One Invisible, are all evidence of his being lately, as it were, a visitant in a higher state of things. I would only have a person reflect on the earnestness and awe with which a child listens to any description or tale, or again, his freedom from that spirit of proud independence, which discovers itself in the soul as time goes on. And though, doubtless, children are generally of a weak and irritable nature, and all are not equally amiable, yet their passions go and are over like a shower, not interfering with the lesson we may gain to our own profit from their ready faith and guilelessness.

The distinctness with which the conscience of a child tells him the difference between right and wrong should also be mentioned. As persons advance in life, and yield to the temptations which come upon them, they lose this original endowment and are obliged to grope about, in many cases because they have lost, through sinning, a guide which they originally had from God. Hence it is that St. John speaks of Christ's undefiled servants as they who "follow the Lamb wherever he goes" (Rev 14:4). They have the minds of children, and are able by the light within them to decide questions of duty at once, undisturbed by the perplexity of discordant arguments.

St. John says, "He who does right is righteous" (1 Jn 3:7), and, again, "Everyone who does right is born of him" (1 Jn 2:29). Now, it is plain a child's innocence has no share in this higher blessedness. He is but a type of what is at length to be fulfilled in him. The chief beauty of his mind is on its mere surface; and when, as time goes on, he attempts to act (as is his duty to do), instantly it disappears. It is only while he is still, that he is like tranquil water, reflecting heaven. Therefore, we must not lament that our youthful days are gone, or sigh over the remembrances of pure pleasures and contemplations which we cannot recall; rather, what we were when children is a blessed intimation, given for our comfort, of what God will make us, if we surrender our hearts to the guidance of his Holy Spirit, a prophecy of good to come, a foretaste of what will be fulfilled in heaven. And thus it is that a child is a pledge of immortality, for he bears upon him in figure those high and eternal excellences in which the joy of heaven consists, and which would not be thus shadowed forth by the all-gracious Creator, were they not one day to be realized.

As then we would one day reign with them, let us in this world learn the mind of little children, as St. John described it: "Little children, let us not love in word or speech, but in deed and in truth" (1 Jn 3:18). "Beloved, let us love one another; for love is of God, and he who loves is born of God and knows God. He who does not love does not know God; for God is love" (1 Jn 4:7-8).

December 29

St. Thomas Becket

Remembrance of Past Mercies

Jacob's distinguishing grace was a habit of affectionate musing upon God's providences towards him in times past, and of overflowing thankfulness for them. Not that he had not other graces also, but this seems to have been his distinguishing grace. All good men have in their measure all graces, for he, by whom they have any, does not give one apart from the whole. He gives the root, and the root puts forth branches. But since time and circumstances and their own use of the gift, and their own disposition and character, have much influence on the mode of its manifestation, so it happens that each good man has his own distinguishing grace, apart from the rest.

Abraham, for instance, Jacob's forefather, was the pattern of faith. This is insisted upon in Scripture, and it is not here necessary to show that he was so. It will be sufficient to say that he left his country at God's word, and, at the same word, took up the knife to slay his own son. Abraham seems to have had something very noble and magnanimous about him. He could realize and make present to him things unseen. He followed God in the dark as promptly, as firmly, with as cheerful a heart, and bold a stepping, as if he were in broad daylight.

Now that faith in which Abraham excelled was not Jacob's characteristic excellence. Not that he had not faith, and great faith, else he would not have been so dear to God. His buying the birthright and gaining the blessing from Esau were proofs of faith. Esau saw nothing or little precious in them. He easily parted with the one, and had no high ideas of the other.

However, Jacob's faith, earnest and vigorous as it was, was not like Abraham's. Abraham, from the first, felt that God was his portion and his inheritance, and, in a great and generous spirit, he freely gave up all he had, being sure that he should find what was more excellent in doing so. But Jacob, in spite of his really living by faith, wished, as one passage of his history shows, to see before he fully believed. When he was escaping from Esau and came to Bethel, and God appeared to him in a dream and gave him promises, but not yet the performance of them, what did he do? Did he simply accept them? He says, "If God will be with me, and will keep me in this way that I go, and will give me bread to eat, and clothing to wear, so that I come again to my father's house in peace, then the Lord shall be my God" (Gn 28:20-21). He makes his obedience, in some sense, depend on a condition; and although we must not, and need not, take the words as if he meant that he would not serve God till and unless he did for him what he had promised, yet they seem to show a fear and anxiety, gentle indeed, and subdued, and very human, yet an anxiety which Abraham had not. We feel Jacob to be more like ourselves than Abraham was.

Jacob seems to have had a gentle, tender, affectionate, timid mind: easily frightened, easily agitated, loving God so much that he feared to lose him, and, like St. Thomas perhaps, anxious for sight and possession from earnest and longing desire of them. Were it not for faith, love would become impatient, and thus Jacob desired to possess, not from cold incredulity or hardness of heart, but from such a loving impatience. Such men are easily downcast and must be treated kindly; they soon despond, they shrink from the world, for they feel its rudeness, which bolder natures do not. Neither Abraham nor Jacob loved the world. But Abraham did not fear, did not feel it. Jacob felt and winced, as being wounded by it. You recollect his touching complaints, "All this has come upon me" (Gn 42:36). "You would bring down my gray hairs with sorrow to Sheol" (Gn 42:38). "If I am bereaved of my children, I am bereaved" (Gn 43:14). You see what a child-like, sensitive, sweet mind he had. Accordingly, his happiness lay, not in looking forward to the hope, but backwards upon the experience, of God's mercies towards him. He delighted lovingly to trace, and gratefully to acknowledge, what had been given, leaving the future to itself.

Well were it for us, if we had the character of mind instanced in Jacob: the temper of dependence upon God's providence, and thankfulness under it, and careful memory of all he had done for us. It would be well if we were in the habit of looking at all we have as God's gift, undeservedly given, and day by day continued to us solely by his mercy. He gave; he may take away. He gave us all we have: life, health, strength, reason, enjoyment, the light of conscience, whatever we have good and holy within us, whatever faith we have, whatever of a renewed will, whatever love towards him, whatever power over ourselves, whatever prospect of heaven. He gave us relatives, friends, education, training, knowledge, the Bible, the Church. All comes from him. He gave; he may take away. Did he take away, we should be called on to follow Job's pattern, and be resigned: "The Lord gave, and the Lord has taken away; blessed be the name of the Lord" (1:21). While he continues his blessings, we should follow Jacob, by living in constant praise and thanksgiving, and in offering up to him of his own.

Let us then view God's providences towards us more religiously than we have hitherto done. Let us try to gain a truer view of what we are, and where we are, in his kingdom. Let us humbly and reverently attempt to trace his guiding hand in the years which we have hitherto lived. Let us thankfully commemorate the many mercies he has granted to us in time past, the many sins he has not remembered, the many dangers he has averted, the many prayers he has answered, the many mistakes he has corrected, the many warnings, the many lessons, the much light, the abounding comfort which he has from time to time given. Let us dwell upon times and seasons, times of trouble, times of joy, times of trial, times of refreshment. How did he cherish us as children! How did he guide us in that dangerous time when the mind begins to think for itself, and the heart to open to the world! How did he with his sweet discipline restrain our passions, mortify our hopes, calm our fears, enliven our heaviness, sweeten our desolateness, and strengthen our infirmities! How did he gently guide us towards the straight gate! How did he allure us along his everlasting way, in spite of its strictness, in spite of its loneliness, in spite of the dim twilight in which it lay! He has been all things to us.

December 30

The Church and the World

Man was made rational, after he was made corporeal. "The LORD God formed man of dust from the ground, and breathed into his nostrils the breath of life; and man became a living soul" (Gn 2:7). Here are two acts on the part of the Creator: the forming the dust, and the breathing the life. Man is confessedly formed on the same mold as other animals. And unbelievers, in consequence, have been so bold as to assert that he does not really differ from them; and because he is outwardly like them, and has an organized body, and can be treated by medical art, as if he were but a framework of matter, and is obliged to employ his brain as an instrument of thought, that in consequence, he has not a soul.

And the case is the same as regards the sacraments of the Gospel. God does not make for us new and miraculous instruments wherewith to convey his benefits, but he adopts means already existing. He takes water, which already is the means of natural health and purity, and consecrates it to convey spiritual life. He changes the use of it. Again, he selects bread and wine, the chief means and symbols of bodily nourishment: he takes them, he blesses them, he does not dispense with them, but he uses them. He leaves them in appearance what they were, but he gifts them with a divine presence, which before they had not. As he filled the Jewish temple of wood and stone with glory on its consecration, as he breathed the breath of life into the dust of the earth, and made it man, so he comes down in power on his chosen symbols, weak though they are in themselves, and makes them what they were not.

Now, from what has been said, this lesson may be learnt: that things of this world are only valuable so far as God's presence is in them, so far as he has breathed on them. In themselves they are but dust and vanity.

When we go into the details of life, the same truth comes upon us forcibly and convincingly. The world is always "in the power of the evil one" (1 Jn 5:19), but we are accustomed sufficiently to admit the faults of former times, which do not concern us; we do not see what is evil in our own. Therefore, we need to be reminded of it. We need to be reminded that all our daily pursuits and doings need not be proved evil, but are certainly evil without proof, unless they can be proved to be good. Unless that holy and superhuman influence which came forth from Christ when he breathed on the apostles, which they handed onwards, which has ever since gone through the world like a leaven, renewing it in righteousness, which came on us first in baptism, and reclaimed us from the service of Satan, unless this divine gift has been cherished and improved within us, and is spread round about and from us, upon the objects of our aims and exertions, upon our plans and pursuits, our words and our works, surely all these are evil, without being formally proved to be so. If we engage in a trade or profession, if we make money, if we form connections in life, if we marry or settle, if we educate our children, whatever we do, we have no right to take it for granted that this is not earthly, sensual, and of this world. It will be so without our trouble, unless we take trouble the other way, unless we aim and pray that it may not be so.

In all things, then, we must spiritualize this world. And if you ask for instances how to do this, I give you the following.

When a nation enters Christ's Church, and takes her yoke upon its shoulder, then it formally joins itself to the cause of God, and separates itself from the evil world. When the civil magistrate defends the Christian faith, and sets it up in all honor in high places, as a beacon to the world, so far he gives himself to God, and sanctifies and spiritualizes that portion of it over which he has power. When men put aside a portion of their gains for God's service, then they sanctify those gains. When the head of a household observes family prayer and other religious offices, and shows that, like Abraham, he is determined with God's help to honor Him, then he joins himself to the kingdom of God, and rescues his household from its natural relationship with this unprofitable world. When a man hallows in his private conduct holy seasons, this is offering up of God's gifts to God, and sanctifying all seasons by the sacrifice of some. When a man who is rich, and whose duty calls on him to be hospitable, is careful also to feed the hungry and clothe the naked, thus he sanctifies his riches. When he is in the midst of plenty, and observes self-denial; when he builds his house, but builds churches too; when he plants and sows, but pays tithes; when he buys and sells, but also gives largely to religion; when he does nothing in the world without being suspicious of the world, being jealous of himself, trying himself, lest he be seduced by the world, making sacrifices to prove his earnestness: in all these ways he circumcises himself from the world by the circumcision of Christ. This is the circumcision of the heart from the world. This is deliverance from dead ordinances; and though, even if this were done perfectly, it would not be enough, for we have to separate ourselves from the flesh also, yet, at least, it is the victory over a chief and formidable adversary.

This is no matter of words, a thing to be listened to carelessly, because we have heard it often before. The death and resurrection of Christ is ever a call upon you to die to time, and to live to eternity. Do not be satisfied with the state in which you find yourselves; do not be satisfied with nature. Be satisfied only with grace. Beware of taking up a low standard of duty, and aiming at nothing but what you can easily fulfil. Pray God to enlighten you with a knowledge of the extent of your duty, to enlighten you with a true view of this world. Beware lest the world seduce you. It will aim at persuading you that it is rational and sensible, that religion is very well in its way, but that we are born for the world. And you will be seduced most certainly, unless you watch and pray that you enter not into temptation. You must either conquer the world, or the world will conquer you. You must be either master or slave. Take your part. "For freedom Christ has set us free; stand fast therefore, and do not submit again to a yoke of slavery" (Gal 5:1).

December 31

St. Sylvester

The Greatness and Littleness of Human Life

Our earthly life gives promise of what it does not accomplish. It promises immortality, yet it is mortal. It contains life in death and eternity in time, and it attracts us by beginnings which faith alone brings to an end. I mean, when we take into account the powers with which our souls are gifted as Christians, the very consciousness of these fills us with a certainty that they must last beyond this life. That is in the case of good and holy men, whose present state is to them who know them well an earnest of immortality. The greatness of their gifts, contrasted with their scanty time for exercising them, forces the mind forward to the thought of another life, as almost the necessary counterpart and consequence of this life, and certainly implied in this life, provided there be a righteous governor of the world who does not make men for naught.

The very greatness of our powers makes this life look pitiful; the very pitifulness of this life forces on our thoughts to another; and the prospect of another gives a dignity and value to this life which promises it. Thus, this life is at once great and little, and we rightly condemn it while we exalt its importance.

And, if this life is short, even when longest, from the great disproportion between it and the powers of regenerate man, still more is this the case, of course, where it is cut short and death comes prematurely. Men there are, who, in a single moment of their lives, have shown a superhuman height and majesty of mind which it would take ages for them to employ on its proper objects, and, as it were, to exhaust; and who by such passing flashes, like rays of the sun, and the darting of lightning, give token of their immortality, give token to us that they are but angels in disguise, the elect of God sealed for eternal life and destined to judge the world and to reign with Christ forever. Yet they are suddenly taken away, and we have hardly recognized them when we lose them. Can we believe that they are not removed for higher things elsewhere? This is sometimes said with reference to our intellectual powers, but it is still more true of our moral nature. There is something in moral truth and goodness, in faith, in firmness, in heavenly-mindedness, in meekness, in courage, in loving-kindness, to which this world's circumstances are quite unequal, for which the longest life is insufficient, which makes the highest opportunities of this world disappointing, which must burst the prison of this world to have its appropriate range. So that when a good man dies, one is led to say, "He has not half showed himself; he has had nothing to exercise him; his days are gone like a shadow, and he is withered like the grass."

Such being the unprofitableness of this life, viewed in itself, it is plain how we should regard it while we go through it. We should remember that it is scarcely more than an accident of our being; that it is no part of ourselves, who are immortal; that we are immortal spirits, independent of time and space, and that this life is but a sort of outward stage on which we act for a time, and which is only sufficient and only intended to answer the purpose of trying whether we will serve God or no. We should consider ourselves to be in this world in no fuller sense than players in any game are in the game, and life to be a sort of dream, as detached and as different from our real eternal existence as a dream differs from waking; a serious dream, indeed, as affording a means of judging us, yet in itself a kind of shadow without substance, a scene set before us, in which we seem to be, and in which it is our duty to act just as if all we saw had a truth and reality, because all that meets us influences us and our destiny.

Let us then thus account for our present state: it is precious to us as revealing to us, amid shadows and figures, the existence and attributes of Almighty God and his elect people. It is precious, because it enables us to hold intercourse with immortal souls who are on their trial as we are. It is momentous, as being the scene and means of our trial. But beyond this it has no claims upon us. "Vanity of vanities," says the preacher, "all is vanity" (Eccl 1:2). We may be poor or rich, young or old, honored or slighted, and it ought to affect us no more, neither to elate us nor depress us, than if we were actors in a play who know that the characters they represent are not their own, and that though they appear to be superior one to another, to be kings or to be peasants, they are in reality all on one level. The one desire which should move us should be, first of all, that of seeing him face to face who is now hid from us, and next of enjoying eternal and direct communion, in and through him, with our friends around us whom at present we know only through the medium of sense, by precarious and partial channels which give us little insight into their hearts.

These are suitable feelings towards this attractive but deceitful world. What have we to do with its gifts and honors, who, having already been baptized into the world to come, are no longer citizens of this? Why should we be anxious for a long life, or wealth, or credit, or comfort, who know that the next world will be everything which our hearts can wish, and that not in appearance only, but truly and everlastingly? Why should we rest in this world, when it is the token and promise of another? Why should we be content with its surface, instead of appropriating what is stored beneath it? To those who live by faith, everything they see speaks of that future world: the very glories of nature, the sun, moon, and stars, and the richness and the beauty of the earth are as types and figures witnessing and teaching the invisible things of God. All that we see is destined one day to burst forth into a heavenly bloom and to be transfigured into immortal glory. Heaven at present is out of sight, but in due time, as snow melts and discovers what it lay upon, so will this visible creation fade away before those greater splendors which are behind it, and on which at present it depends.

These are the thoughts to make us eagerly and devoutly say, "Come, Lord Jesus, to end the time of waiting, of darkness, of turbulence, of disputing, of sorrow, of care." These are the thoughts to lead us to rejoice in every day and hour that passes, as bringing us nearer the time of his appearing and the termination of sin and misery. May he grant his grace abundantly to us, to make us meet for his presence, that we may not be ashamed before him at his coming! May he grant us the full grace of his ordinances; may he feed us with his choicest gifts; may he expel the poison from our souls; may he wash us clean in his precious blood and give us the fulness of faith, love, and hope, as foretastes of the heavenly portion which he destines for us!

January 1
Mary, the Mother of God

The Mystery of Divine Condescension

You say that God and man never can be one, that man cannot bear the sight and touch of his Creator, nor the Creator condescend to the feebleness of the creature; but blush and be confounded to hear, O peevish, restless hearts, that he has come down from his high throne and humbled himself to the creature, in order that the creature might be inspired and strengthened to rise to him.

It was not enough to give man grace; it was little to impart to him a celestial light, and a sanctity such as angels had received, little to create Adam in original justice, with a heavenly nature superadded to his own, with an intellect which could know God and a soul which could love him. He purposed even in man's first state of innocence a higher mercy, which in the fulness of time was to be accomplished on his behalf. It became the Wisdom of God, who is the eternally glorious and beautiful, to impress these attributes upon men by his very presence and personal indwelling in their flesh, that, as he was by nature the only-begotten image of the Father, so he might also become "the first-born of all creation" (Col 1:15). It became him who is higher than the highest to act as if even humility, if this dare be said, was in the number of his attributes, by taking Adam's nature upon himself and manifesting himself to men and angels in it.

Your God has taken on him your nature. Now prepare yourself to see in human flesh that glory and that beauty on which the angels gaze. Since you are to see Emmanuel, since the brilliancy of the Eternal Light and the "spotless mirror" of

God's majesty, and the "image of his goodness" (cf. Wis 7:26) is to walk the earth, since the Son of the Highest is to be born of woman, since the manifold attributes of the Infinite are to be poured out before your eyes through material channels and the operations of a human soul, since he, whose contemplation did but trouble you in nature, is coming to take you captive by a manifestation which is both intelligible to you and a pledge that he loves you one by one, raise high your expectations, for surely they cannot suffer disappointment. Doubtless, you will say, he will take a form such as "no eye has seen, nor ear heard" before (1 Cor 2:9). It will be a body framed in the heavens, and only committed to the custody of Mary; a form of light and glory, worthy of him who is "blessed forever" (2 Cor 11:31) and comes to bless us with his presence. Pomp and pride of men he may indeed despise. We do not look for him in kings' courts, or in the array of war, or in the philosophic school, but doubtless he will choose some calm and holy spot, and men will go out thither and find their Incarnate God. He will be tenant of some paradise, like Adam or Elijah, or he will dwell in the mystic garden of the Canticles, where nature ministers its best and purest to its Creator. "The fig tree," will put forth "its green figs," the vines in flower will "give forth fragrance" (Sg 2:13). "Nard and saffron" will be there, "calamus and cinnamon, with all trees of frankincense, myrrh and aloes, with all chief spices" (Sg 4:14), before the glory of the Lord and the beauty of our God. There will he show himself at stated times, with angels for his choristers and saints for his doorkeepers, to the poor and needy, to the humble and devout, to those who have kept their innocence undefiled, or have purged their sins away by long penance and masterful contrition.

Such would be the conjecture of man, at fault when he speculates on the height of God as when he tries to sound the depth. He thinks that a royal glory is the note of his presence

upon earth. Lift up your eyes, my brethren, and answer whether
he has guessed aright. Oh, incomprehensible in eternity and
in time! "Who is this, that comes from Edom, in crimsoned
garments from Bozrah?...why is your apparel red, and your
garments like his who treads in the wine press?" (Is 63:1-2). It
is because the Maker of man, the Wisdom of God, has come,
not in strength, but in weakness.

He has come, not to assert a claim, but to pay a debt. Instead
of wealth, he has come poor; instead of honor, he has come
in ignominy; instead of blessedness, he has come to suffer. He
has been delivered over from his birth to pain and contempt.
His delicate frame is worn down by cold and heat, by hunger
and sleeplessness. His hands are rough and bruised with a
mechanic's toil. His eyes are dimmed with weeping. His name
is cast out as evil. He is flung amid the throng of men. He
wanders from place to place. He is the companion of sinners.
He is followed by a mixed multitude, who care more for meat
and drink than for his teaching, or by a city's populace which
deserts him in the day of trial. And at length he who "reflects
the glory of God and bears the very stamp of his nature" (Heb
1:3 DR) is fettered, shoved to and fro, buffeted, spit upon,
mocked, cursed, scourged, and tortured. "He had no form or
comeliness . . . he was despised and rejected by men; a man of
sorrows, and acquainted with grief," nay, he is a man "struck
down by God, and afflicted" (Is 53:2-4). And so his clothes are
torn off, and he is lifted up upon the bitter cross, and there he
hangs, a spectacle for profane, impure, and savage eyes, and a
mockery for the evil spirit whom he had cast down into hell.

O wayward man! Discontented first that thy God is far from
thee, discontented again when he has drawn near. Complaining
first that he is high, complaining next that he is low! Unhumbled
being, when will you cease to make yourself your own center,
and learn that God is infinite in all he does, infinite when he

reigns in heaven, infinite when he serves on earth, exacting our homage in the midst of his angels, and winning homage from us in the midst of sinners? Adorable he is in his eternal rest, adorable in the glory of his court, adorable in the beauty of his works, most adorable of all, most royal, most persuasive in his deformity. Think you not that to Mary, when she held him in her maternal arms, when she gazed on the pale countenance and the dislocated limbs of her God, when she traced the wandering lines of blood, when she counted the welts, the bruises, and the wounds which dishonored that virginal flesh, think you not that to her eyes it was more beautiful than when she first worshipped it—pure, radiant, and fragrant—on the night of his nativity?

January 2

Saints Basil and Gregory

Warfare the Condition of Victory

"He who conquers, I will grant him to sit with me on my throne, as I myself conquered and sat down with my Father on his throne" (Rev 3:21). It will be well if we take this lesson to ourselves, and learn that great truth which the apostles shrank from at first, but at length rejoiced in. Christ suffered and entered into joy; so did they, in their measure, after him. And in our measure, so do we. It is written that "through many tribulations we must enter the kingdom of God" (Acts 14:22). God has all things in his own hands. He can spare, he can inflict. He often spares (may he spare us still!), but he often tries us; in one way or another he tries every one. At some time or other of the life of every one there is pain, and sorrow, and trouble. So it is. And the sooner perhaps we can look upon it as a law of our Christian condition, the better. One generation comes, and then another. They issue forth and succeed like leaves in spring; and in all, this law is observable. They are tried, and then they triumph. They are humbled, and then are exalted. They overcome the world, and then they sit down on Christ's throne.

Hence St. Peter, who at first was in such amazement and trouble at his Lord's afflictions, bids us not look on suffering as a strange thing, "as though something strange were happening to you. But rejoice in so far as you share Christ's sufferings, that you may also rejoice and be glad when his glory is revealed" (1 Pet 4:12-13). Again, St. Paul says, "We rejoice in our sufferings, knowing that suffering produces endurance" (Rom 5:3). And again, "If we endure, we shall also reign with him"

(2 Tm 2:12). What is here said of persecution will apply of course to all trials, and much more to those lesser trials which are the utmost which Christians have commonly to endure now. Yet I suppose it is a long time before any one of us recognizes and understands that his own state on earth is in one shape or other a state of trial and sorrow; and that if he has intervals of external peace, this is all gain, and more than he has a right to expect. The heavenly hosts, who see what is going on upon earth, well understand, even from having seen it often, what is the course of a soul traveling from hell to heaven. They have seen, again and again, in numberless instances, that suffering is the path to peace, that they who sow in tears shall reap in joy, and that what was true of Christ is fulfilled in a measure in his followers.

Let us try to accustom ourselves to this view of the subject. The whole Church, all elect souls, each in its turn, is called to this necessary work. Once it was the turn of others, now it is our turn. Once it was the apostles' turn. It was St. Paul's turn once. He had all cares on him all at once, covered from head to foot with cares, as Job with sores. And, as if all this were not enough, he had a thorn in the flesh added. Yet he did his part well; he was as a strong and bold wrestler in his day, and at the close of it was able to say, "I have fought the good fight, I have finished the race, I have kept the faith" (2 Tm 4:7). And after him, the excellent of the earth, the white-robed army of martyrs and the cheerful company of confessors, each in his turn, each in his day, have likewise played the man. And so down to this very time, when faith has well-nigh faded, first one and then another have been called out to exhibit before the Great King.

Such is our state. Angels are looking on. Christ has gone before. Christ has given us an example that we may follow his steps. He went through far more, infinitely more, than we can be called to suffer. Our brethren have gone through much more, and they seem to encourage us by their success. Now it is our turn, and all ministering spirits keep silence and look on. O let not your foot slip, or your eye be false, or your ear dull, or your attention flagging! Be not dispirited; be not afraid; keep a good heart; be bold; draw not back: you will be carried through. Whatever troubles come on you, of mind, body, or estate, from within or from without, from chance or from intent, from friends or foes, whatever your trouble be, though you be lonely, O children of a heavenly Father, be not afraid! Acquit yourselves like men in your day, and when it is over, Christ will receive you to himself, and your heart shall rejoice, and your joy no man shall take from you.

Christ is already in that place of peace, which is all in all. He is on the right hand of God. He is hidden in the brightness of the radiance which issues from the everlasting throne. He is in the very abyss of peace, where there is no voice of tumult or distress, but a deep stillness—stillness, that great and most awful of all goods which we can fancy—that most perfect of joys, the utter, profound, ineffable tranquility of the divine essence. He has entered into his rest.

O how great a good will it be, if, when this troublesome life is over, we in our turn also enter into that same rest, if the time shall one day come, when we shall enter into his tabernacle above, and hide ourselves under the shadow of his wings; if we shall be in the number of those blessed dead who die in the Lord and rest from their labor. Here we are tossing upon the sea, and the wind is contrary. All through the day we are tried and tempted in various ways. We cannot think, speak, act, but infirmity and sin are at hand. But in the unseen world, where Christ has entered, all is peace.

That is our home; here we are but on pilgrimage, and Christ is calling us home. He calls us to his many mansions which he has prepared. And the Spirit calls us too, and all things will be ready for us by the time of our coming. Seeing then that "we have a great high priest who has passed through the heavens, Jesus, the Son of God, let us hold fast our confession" (Heb 4:14); seeing we have "so great a cloud of witnesses, let us also lay aside every weight" (Heb 12:1); "let us therefore strive to enter that rest" (Heb 4:11); and, "let us then with confidence draw near to the throne of grace, that we may receive mercy and find grace to help in time of need" (Heb 4:16).

January 3

Affliction, a School of Comfort

If there is one point of character more than another which belonged to St. Paul, and discovers itself in all he said and did, it was his power of sympathizing with his brethren, nay, with all classes of men. He went through trials of every kind, and this was their issue, to let him into the feelings, and thereby to introduce him to the hearts, of high and low, Jew and Gentile. He knew how to persuade, for he knew where lay the perplexity; he knew how to console, for he knew the sorrow. His spirit within him was as some delicate instrument, which, as the weather changed about him, as the atmosphere was moist or dry, hot or cold, accurately marked all its variations and guided him what to do. To the Jews he became as a Jew, that he might gain the Jews; to them that were under the Law, as under the Law, that he might gain them that were under the Law; to them that were without Law, as without Law, that he might gain them that were without Law. "To the weak," he says, "I became weak, that I might win the weak. I have become all things to all men, that I might by all means save some" (1 Cor 9:20-22). And so again, in another place, after having recounted his various trials by sea and land, in the bleak wilderness and the stifling prison, from friends and strangers, he adds, "Who is weak, and I am not weak? Who is made to fall, and I am not indignant? If I must boast, I will boast of the things that show my weakness" (2 Cor 11:29-30). He himself gives the reason for his trials, speaking of Almighty God's comforting him in all his tribulation, in order that he might be able to comfort them which were in any trouble, by the comfort wherewith he himself was comforted by God (cf. 2 Cor 1:4).

Now, in speaking of the benefits of trial and suffering, we should of course never forget that these things by themselves have no power to make us holier or more heavenly. They make many men morose, selfish, and envious. The only sympathy they create in many minds is the wish that others should suffer with them, not they with others. Affliction, when love is away, leads a man to wish others to be as he is; it leads to repining, malevolence, hatred, rejoicing in evil. "You too have become as weak as we! You have become like us!" (Is 14:10), said the princes of the nations to the fallen king of Babylon. The devils are not incited by their own torments to any endeavor but that of making others devils also. Such is the effect of pain and sorrow, when unsanctified by God's saving grace. And this is instanced very widely and in a variety of cases. All afflictions of the flesh, such as the Gospel enjoins, and St. Paul practiced, watching and fastings, and subjecting of the body, have no tendency whatever in themselves to make men better. They often have made men worse. They often—to appearance—have left them just as they were before. They are no sure test of holiness and true faith, taken by themselves.

It should ever be borne in mind that the severest and most mortified life is as little a passport to heaven, or a criterion of saintliness, as benevolence is, or usefulness, or amiableness. Self-discipline is a necessary condition, but not a sure sign of holiness. It may leave a man worldly, or it may make him a tyrant. It is only in the hands of God that it is God's instrument. It only ministers to God's purposes when God uses it. It is only when grace is in the heart, when power from above dwells in a man, that anything outward or inward turns to his salvation. Whether persecution, or famine, or the sword, they as little bring the soul to Christ as they separate it from him. He alone can work, and he can work through all things. He can make the stones bread. He can feed us with every word which proceeds from his mouth. He could, did he so will, make us calm, resigned, tender-hearted, and sympathizing, without trial, but it is his will ordinarily to do so by means of trial. Even he himself, when he came on earth, condescended to gain knowledge by experience, and what he did himself, that he makes his brethren do.

Almighty God chose worldly trial as the portion of his saints, and sanctified it by his heavenly grace to be their great benefit. He rescues them from the selfishness of worldly comfort without surrendering them to the selfishness of worldly pain. He brings them into pain, that they may be like what Christ was, and may be led to think of him, not of themselves. He brings them into trouble, that they may be near him. When they mourn, they are more intimately in his presence than they are at any other time. Bodily pain, anxiety, bereavement, distress, are to them his forerunners.

Taught by our own pain, our own sorrow, nay, by our own sin, we shall have hearts and minds exercised for every service of love towards those who need it. We shall in our measure be comforters after the image of the Almighty Paraclete, and that in all senses of the word: advocates, assistants, soothing aids. Our words and advice, our very manner, voice, and look, will be gentle and tranquilizing, as of those who have borne their cross after Christ. We shall not pass by his little ones rudely, as the world does. The voice of the widow and the orphan, the poor and destitute, will at once reach our ears, however low they speak. Our hearts will open towards them; our word and deed befriend them. The ruder passions of man's nature—pride and anger, envy and strife—which so disorder the Church, these will be quelled and brought under in others by the earnestness and kindness of our admonitions.

Thus, instead of being the selfish creatures which we were by nature, grace, acting through suffering, tends to make us ready teachers and witnesses to Truth. Time was when, even at the most necessary times, we found it difficult to speak of heaven to another, our mouth seemed closed, even when our heart was full; but now our affection is eloquent, and "out of the abundance of the heart" (Lk 6:45) our mouth speaks. Blessed portion indeed, thus to be tutored in the sweetest, softest strains of Gospel truth, and to range over the face of the earth pilgrims and sojourners, with winning voices, singing, as far as in the flesh it is possible to sing, the song of Moses the servant of God and the song of the Lamb, severed from ties of earth by the trials we have endured, without father, without mother, without abiding place, as that patriarch whom St. Paul speaks of, and, like him, allowed to bring forth bread and wine to refresh the weary soldiers of the most high God.

St. Elizabeth Ann Seton

The Thought of God, the Stay of the Soul

By birth we are in a state of defect and want; we have not all that is necessary for the perfection of our nature. As the body is not complete in itself, but requires the soul to give it a meaning, so again the soul till God is present with it and manifested in it, has faculties and affections without a ruling principle, object, or purpose. Such it is by birth, and this Scripture signifies to us by many figures—sometimes calling human nature blind, sometimes hungry, sometimes unclothed, and calling the gift of the Spirit light, health, food, warmth, and raiment—all by way of teaching us what our first state is, and what our gratitude should be to him who has brought us into a new state. For instance, "Awake, O sleeper, and arise from the dead, and Christ shall give you light" (Eph 5:14). Again, "Whoever drinks of the water that I shall give him will never thirst; the water that I shall give him will become in him a spring of water welling up to eternal life" (Jn 4:14). And in the book of Psalms, "They feast on the abundance of your house, and you give them drink from the river of your delights. For with you is the fountain of life; in your light do we see light" (Ps 36:8-9).

Now the doctrine which these passages contain is often truly expressed thus: that the soul of man is made for the contemplation of its Maker, and that nothing short of that high contemplation is its happiness.

The happiness of the soul consists in the exercise of the affections—not in sensual pleasures, not in activity, not in excitement, not in self-esteem, not in the consciousness of power, not in knowledge—in none of these things lies our happiness, but in our affections being elicited, employed, supplied. As hunger and thirst, as taste, sound, and smell, are the channels through which this bodily frame receives pleasure, so the affections are the instruments by which the soul has pleasure. When they are exercised duly, it is happy; when they are undeveloped, restrained, or thwarted, it is not happy. This is our real and true bliss, not to know, or to affect, or to pursue, but to love, to hope, to joy, to admire, to revere, to adore. Our real and true bliss lies in the possession of those objects on which our hearts may rest and be satisfied.

Now, if this be so, here is at once a reason for saying that the thought of God, and nothing short of it, is the happiness of man, for though there is much besides to serve as subject of knowledge, or motive for action, or means of excitement, yet the affections require something more vast and more enduring than anything created. What is novel and sudden excites, but does not influence; what is pleasurable or useful raises no awe; self moves no reverence, and mere knowledge kindles no love. He who made it is alone sufficient for the heart. I do not say, of course, that nothing short of the Almighty Creator can awaken and answer to our love, reverence, and trust; man can do this for man. Man doubtless is an object to rouse his brother's love, and repays it in his measure. Nay, it is a great duty, one of the two chief duties of religion, thus to be minded towards our neighbor. But I am not speaking here of what we can do, or ought to do, but what it is our happiness to do. And surely it may be said that though the love of the brethren, the love of all men, be one half of our obedience, yet exercised by itself—were that possible, which it is not—it would be no part of our reward. And for this reason, if for no other: that our hearts require something more permanent and uniform than man can be. We gain much for a time from fellowship with each other. It is a relief to us, as fresh air to the fainting, or meat and drink to the hungry, or a flood of tears to the heavy in mind. It is a soothing comfort to have those whom we may make our confidants, a comfort to have those to whom we may confess our faults, a comfort to have those to whom we may look for sympathy. Love of home and family in these and other ways is sufficient to make this life tolerable to the multitude of men, which otherwise it would not be; but still, after all, our affections exceed such exercise of them, and demand what is more stable. Do not all men die? Are they not taken from us? Are they not as uncertain as the grass of the field? We do not give our hearts to things irrational, because these have no permanence in them. We do not place our affections in sun, moon, and stars, or this rich and fair earth, because all things material come to naught, and vanish like day and night.

There is another reason why God alone is the happiness of our souls: the contemplation of him, and nothing but it, is able fully to open and relieve the mind, to unlock, occupy, and fix our affections. We may indeed love things created with great intensity, but such affection, when disjoined from the love of the Creator, is like a stream running in a narrow channel, impetuous, vehement, turbid. The heart runs out, as it were, only at one door; it is not an expanding of the whole man. Created natures cannot open us, or elicit the ten thousand mental senses which belong to us, and through which we really live. None but the presence of our Maker can enter us, for to none besides can the whole heart in all its thoughts and feelings be unlocked and subjected. "Behold," he says, "I stand at the door and knock; if any one hears my voice and opens the door, I will come in to him, and eat with him, and he with me" (Rev 3:20). "My Father will love him, and we will come to him, and make our home with him" (Jn 14:23). "God has sent the Spirit of his Son into our hearts" (Gal 4:6). "God is greater than our hearts, and he knows everything" (1 Jn 3:20). It is this feeling of simple and absolute confidence and communion which soothes and satisfies those to whom it is given.

Life passes, riches fly away, popularity is fickle, the senses decay, the world changes, friends die. One alone is constant. One alone is true to us. One alone can be true. One alone can be all things to us. One alone can supply our needs. One alone can train us up to our full perfection. One alone can give a meaning to our complex and intricate nature. One alone can give us tune and harmony. One alone can form and possess us. Are we allowed to put ourselves under his guidance? This surely is the only question. Has he really made us his children, and taken possession of us by his Holy Spirit? Are we still in his kingdom of grace, in spite of our sins? The question is not whether we should go, but whether he will receive. And we trust, that, in spite of our sins, he will receive us still, every one of us, if we seek his face in love unfeigned, and holy fear. Let us then do our part, as he has done his, and much more. Let us say with the Psalmist, "Whom have I in heaven but you? And there is nothing upon earth that I desire besides you. My flesh and my heart may fail, but God is the strength of my heart and my portion forever" (Ps 73:25-6).

January 5

St. John Neumann

Love, the One Thing Needful

I suppose the greater number of persons who try to live Christian lives, and who observe themselves with any care, are dissatisfied with their own state on this point, namely, that whatever their religious attainments may be, yet they feel that their motive is not the highest, that the love of God, and of man for his sake, is not their ruling principle. They may do much, they may suffer much, but they have little reason to think that they love much, that they do and suffer for love's sake. I do not mean that they thus express themselves exactly, but that they are dissatisfied with themselves, and that when this dissatisfaction is examined into, it will be found ultimately to come to this, though they will give different accounts of it. They may call themselves cold, or hard-hearted, or fickle, or double-minded, or doubting, or dim-sighted, or weak in resolve, but they mean pretty much the same thing: that their affections do not rest on Almighty God as their great object. And this will be found to be the complaint of religious men among ourselves, not less than others, their reason and their heart not going together, their reason tending heavenwards, and their heart earthwards.

Let us consider the continual duties of daily life, and let us see whether these may not be performed with considerable exactness, yet with deficient love. Surely they may, and serious men complain of themselves here. Our Lord says, "If you love me, you will keep my commandments" (Jn 14:15), but they feel that though they are, to a certain point, keeping God's commandments, yet love is not proportionate, does not keep pace, with their obedience; that obedience springs from some source short of love. This they perceive; they feel themselves to be hollow, a fair outside, without a spirit within it.

I mean as follows. It is possible to obey, not from love towards God and man, but from a sort of conscientiousness short of love, from some notion of acting up to a law, that is, more from the fear of God than from love of him. Surely this is what, in one shape or another, we see daily on all sides of us: the case of men, living to the world, yet not without a certain sense of religion which acts as a restraint on them. They pursue ends of this world, but not to the full; they are checked, and go a certain way only, because they dare not go further. This external restraint acts with various degrees of strength on various persons. They all live to this world, and act from love of it; they all allow their love of the world a certain range, but, at some particular point, which is often quite arbitrary, this man stops, and that man stops. Each stops at a different point in the course of the world, and thinks everyone else profane who goes further, and superstitious who does not go so far, laughs at the latter, is shocked at the former.

And what takes place so generally in the world, serious men will feel as happening in its degree in their own case. They will understand that even strict obedience is no evidence of fervent love, and they will lament to perceive that they obey God far more than they love him.

These are some of the proofs which are continually brought home to us, if we attend to ourselves, of our want of love of God. As to the mode of overcoming the evil, I must say plainly this, that, fanciful though it may appear at first sight to say so, the comforts of life are the main cause of it, and, much as we may lament and struggle against it, till we learn to dispense with them in good measure, we shall not overcome it. Till we, in a certain sense, detach ourselves from our bodies, our minds will not be in a state to receive divine impressions, and to exert heavenly aspirations. A smooth and easy life, an uninterrupted enjoyment of the goods of Providence, full meals, soft garments, well-furnished homes, the pleasures of sense, the feeling of security, the consciousness of wealth: these, and the like, if we are not careful, choke up all the avenues of the soul, through which the light and breath of heaven might come to us. A hard life is, alas, no certain method of becoming spiritually minded, but it is one out of the means by which Almighty God makes us so. We must, at least at seasons, defraud ourselves of nature, if we would not be defrauded of grace. If we attempt to force our minds into a loving and devotional temper without this preparation, it is too plain what will follow: the grossness and coarseness, the affectation, the hollowness, in a word, what Scripture calls the hypocrisy, which we see around us, that state of mind in which the reason, seeing what we should be, and the conscience enjoining it, and the heart being unequal to it, some or other pretense is set up, by way of compromise.

And next, after enjoining this habitual preparation of heart, let me bid you cherish a constant sense of the love of your Lord and Savior in dying on the cross for you. Here, again, self-discipline will be necessary. It makes the heart tender as well as reverent. Christ showed his love in deed, not in word, and you will be touched by the thought of his cross far more by bearing it after him, than by glowing accounts of it. All the modes by which you bring it before you must be simple and severe. Think of the cross when you rise and when you lie down, when you go out and when you come in, when you eat and when you walk and when you converse, when you buy and when you sell, when you labor and when you rest, consecrating and sealing all your doings with this one mental action: the thought of the Crucified. Do not talk of it to others. Be silent, like the penitent woman, who showed her love in deep subdued acts. She stood "behind him at his feet, weeping" and "began to wet his feet with her tears, and wiped them with the hair of her head, and kissed his feet, and anointed them with the ointment" (Lk 7:38). And Christ said of her, "Her sins, which are many, are forgiven, for she loved much" (Lk 7:47).

And, further, let us dwell often upon those his manifold mercies to us and to our brethren, which are the consequence of his coming upon earth: his adorable counsels, as manifested in our personal election; the wonders of his grace towards us, from our infancy until now; the gifts he has given us; the aid he has granted; the answers he has accorded to our prayers. And, further, let us, as far as we have the opportunity, meditate upon his dealings with his Church from age to age: on his faithfulness to his promises, and the mysterious mode of their fulfilment; how he has ever led his people forward safely and prosperously on the whole amid so many enemies; what unexpected events have worked his purposes; how evil has been changed into good; how his sacred truth has ever been preserved unimpaired; how saints have been brought on to their perfection in the darkest times. And, further, let us muse over the deep gifts and powers lodged in the Church: what thoughts do his ordinances raise in the believing mind! What wonder, what awe, what transport, when duly dwelt upon!

It is by such deeds and such thoughts that our services, our repenting, our prayers, our conversation with others, will be imbued with the spirit of love. Then we do everything thankfully and joyfully, when we are temples of Christ, with his image set up in us. Then it is that we mix with the world without loving it, for our affections are given to another. We can bear to look on the world's beauty, for we have no heart for it. We are not disturbed at its frowns, for we live not in its smiles. We rejoice in the house of prayer, because he is there whom our soul loves. We can condescend to the poor and lowly, for they are the presence of him who is invisible. We are patient in bereavement, adversity, or pain, for they are Christ's tokens.

January 6

The Epiphany of the Lord

The Season of Epiphany

Epiphany is a season especially set apart for adoring the glory of Christ. The word may be taken to mean the manifestation of his glory, and leads us to the contemplation of him as a king upon his throne in the midst of his court, with his servants around him, and his guards in attendance. At Christmas we commemorate his grace, and in Lent his temptation, and on Good Friday his sufferings and death, and on Easter Day his victory, and on Ascension Thursday his return to the Father, and in Advent we anticipate his second coming. And in all of these seasons he does something, or suffers something, but on Epiphany and the days after it, we celebrate him, not as on his field of battle, or in his solitary retreat, but as an august and glorious king. We view him as the object of our worship. Then only, during his whole earthly history, did he fulfil the type of Solomon, and held a court, and received the homage of his subjects, namely, when he was an infant. His throne was his undefiled mother's arms; his chamber of state was a cottage or a cave; the worshippers were the wise men of the East, and they brought presents, gold, frankincense, and myrrh. All around and about him seemed of earth, except to the eye of faith; one note alone had he of divinity. As great men of this world are often plainly dressed, and look like other men, all but as having some one costly ornament on their breast or on their brow, so the Son of Mary in his lowly dwelling, and in an infant's form, was declared to be the Son of God most high, the Father of ages, and the Prince of Peace, by his star, a wonderful appearance which had guided the wise men all the way from the East, even unto Bethlehem.

The only display of royal greatness, the only season of majesty, homage, and glory, which our Lord had on earth, was in his infancy and youth. Gabriel's message to Mary was in its style and manner such as befitted an angel speaking to Christ's mother. Elizabeth, too, saluted Mary, and the future Baptist his hidden Lord, in the same honorable way. Angels announced his birth, and the shepherds worshipped. A star appeared, and the wise men rose from the East and made him offerings. He was brought to the Temple, and Simeon took him in his arms and returned thanks for him. He grew to twelve years old, and again he appeared in the Temple, and took his seat in the midst of the doctors. But here his earthly majesty had its end, or if seen afterwards, it was but now and then, by glimpses and by sudden gleams, but with no steady sustained light, and no diffused radiance. We are told at the close of the last-mentioned narrative, "And he went down with them and came to Nazareth, and was obedient to them" (Lk 2:51). His subjection and servitude now began in fact. He had come in the form of a servant, and now he took on him a servant's office. How much is contained in the idea of his subjection! And it began, and his time of glory ended, when he was twelve years old.

Solomon, the great type of the Prince of Peace, reigned forty years, and his name and greatness was known far and wide through the East. Joseph, the much-loved son of Jacob, who in an earlier age of the Church was a type of Christ in his kingdom, was in power and favor eighty years, twice as long as Solomon. But Christ, the true revealer of secrets, and the dispenser of the bread of life, the true wisdom and majesty of the Father, manifested his glory but in his early years, and then the Sun of Righteousness was clouded. For he was not to reign really, till he left the world.

It often happens that when persons are in serious illnesses and in delirium in consequence or other disturbance of mind, they have some few minutes of respite in the midst of it, when they are even more than themselves, as if to show us what they really are, and to interpret for us what else would be dreary. And again, some have thought that the minds of children have on them traces of something more than earthly, which fade away as life goes on, but are the promise of what is intended for them hereafter. And somewhat in this way, if we may dare compare ourselves with our gracious Lord, in a parallel though higher way, Christ descends to the shadows of this world, with the transitory tokens on him of that future glory in which he could not enter till he had suffered. The star burned brightly over him for awhile, though it then faded away.

We see the same law, as it may be called, of Divine Providence in other cases also. Consider, for instance, how the prospect of our Lord's passion opens upon the apostles in the sacred history. Where did they hear of it? Moses and Elijah "appeared in glory and spoke of his exodus, which he was to accomplish at Jerusalem" (Lk 9:30-31). That is, the season of his bitter trial was preceded by a short gleam of the glory which was to be, when he was suddenly transfigured, and "the appearance of his countenance was altered, and his clothing became dazzling white" (Lk 9:29). And with this glory in prospect, our Lord abhorred not to die, as it is written: "Who for the joy that was set before him endured the cross, despising the shame" (Heb 12:2).

Let us, then, thankfully cherish all seasons of peace and joy which are granted us here below. Let us beware of abusing them, and of resting in them, of forgetting that they are special privileges, of neglecting to look out for trouble and trial, as our due and our portion. Trial is our portion here; we must not think it strange when trial comes after peace. Still God mercifully does grant a respite now and then; and perhaps he grants it to us the more, the more careful we are not to abuse it. For all seasons we must thank him, for time of sorrow and time of joy, time of warfare and time of peace. And the more we thank him for the one, the more we shall be drawn to thank him for the other. Each has its own proper fruit, and its own peculiar blessedness. Yet our mortal flesh shrinks from the one, and of itself prefers the other. It prefers rest to toil, peace to war, joy to sorrow, health to pain and sickness. When, then, Christ gives us what is pleasant, let us take it as a refreshment by the way, that we may, when God calls, go in the strength of that meat forty days and forty nights unto Horeb, the mount of God. Let us rejoice in Epiphany with trembling, that after the Baptism of the Lord we may go into the vineyard with cheerfulness, and may sorrow in Lent with thankfulness. Let us rejoice now, not as if we have attained, but in hope of attaining. Let us take our present happiness, not as our true rest, but, as what the land of Canaan was to the Israelites, a type and shadow of it. If we now enjoy God's ordinances, let us not cease to pray that they may prepare us for his presence hereafter. If we enjoy the presence of friends, let them remind us of the communion of saints before his throne. Let us trust in nothing here, yet draw hope from everything, that at length the Lord may be our everlasting light, and the days of our mourning ended.